OPERATION SPETSNAZ

OPERATION SPETSNAZ

THE AIMS
TACTICS AND TECHNIQUES OF
SOVIET SPECIAL FORCES

Michael G. Welham · Bruce Quarrie

Patrick Stephens Limited

British Library Cataloguing in Publication Data

Quarrie, Bruce, *1947-*
Operation Spetsnaz: the aims, tactics and techniques of
Soviet special forces.
1. Soviet special forces
I. Title   II. Welham, Michael
356'.160947

ISBN 1-852660-121-3

Patrick Stephens is part of the
Thorsons Publishing Group,
Wellingborough, Northamptonshire,
NN8 2RQ, England.

Photoset in North Wales by
Derek Doyle & Associates Mold, Clwyd
and Printed in Great Britain by
Mackays of Chatham, Kent

1   3   5   7   9   10   8   6   4   2

Contents

Introduction

During the autumn of 1988 the newspapers, radio and television bulletins were full of details regarding the trial in Gibraltar of soldiers from the British Special Air Service Regiment – and by implication, the trial of the regiment itself and the need for its existence.

The soldiers involved in the deaths of Irish Republican Army terrorists eventually received the verdict which most people could have predicted from the outset – and by so doing vindicated their regiment.

Until the much televised and publicised rescue of the hostages in the Iranian Embassy siege, in London in 1980, few people had really heard much about the SAS – 'Ess Ay Ess' to the majority but 'Sass' to its members. Tony Geraghty's fortuitous book *Who Dares Wins*, published immediately after the event, awakened public interest and gave the average person an insight into the regiment's achievements, from its formation in 1942 by the now legendary David Stirling through its activities in the remainder of the Second World War and subsequently in Malaya, Oman, Borneo, Aden, Northern Ireland and elsewhere.

The failure, through no fault of the men concerned, of the American Special Forces Operational Detachment 'Delta', or just 'Delta' for short, to rescue the hostages in Tehran in the same year focused attention still further on the elite forces which have been raised and trained for 'special' missions by most of the world's armed forces and intelligence agencies. Both the Falklands' conflict and the American invasion of Grenada in 1982 further fuelled the fires of speculation and enquiry.

The Special Air Service Regiment is a regular part of the

British Army and draws its recruits from the most able and highly motivated officers and men in the ranks of other regiments – notably the Parachute Regiment. The same is true of the Special Boat Squadron, naval equivalent of the SAS which recruits from the Royal Marines and is in some ways even more highly skilled. 'Delta', formed by Colonel Charlie Beckwith after he had experienced SAS methods and techniques while on secondment during the 1960s, is firmly based on the same principles. So are the elite forces of Israel, which came into the public eye in 1976 at the time of the famous Entebbe raid, or West Germany's GSG9, formed after the Munich Olympic Games massacre and responsible (with SAS help) for the Mogadishu rescue.

If these Western elite forces could have been nurtured in secrecy, though, and only exposed through the media in recent years when their exploits could no longer be hidden, is it any surprise that even fewer people have heard of Spetsnaz?

The *Voyska Spezialnoye Naznachenia*, popularly abbreviated to *Spetsnaz*[1], is the Soviet Union's equivalent of the SAS and SBS, having both airborne and marine elements, although it is larger and must enjoy an appreciably higher budget (even though we are never likely to know the exact size of either). It is a military formation whose very existence is largely unknown within the Soviet Union, or even within the armed forces of Russia and the Warsaw Pact. As explored in the following pages, it is an elite body of rigorously trained and ideologically motivated men (and women) tasked with deep behind the lines reconnaissance missions; with sabotage; with information gathering on both tactical military subjects and technological developments for Soviet military intelligence, the GRU; with helping in the training and, indirectly, the financing of many terrorist groups[2] and left-wing political organizations worldwide, including supplying them with arms and explosives; with liaising with 'sleeper' networks; and with murder.

In a surprising broadcast on Thursday, 6 October 1988, the British Broadcasting Corporation's 'Nine O'Clock News' ran an unheralded item about a Russian delegation sent over to observe British military exercises 'in the south of the country'. They were, the report concluded, particularly interested in watching the British Army's defensive tactics directed against Spetsnaz sabotage teams.

The Soviet delegation comprised four Colonels, one of whom

wore airborne insignia and one naval infantry. They arrived after a mere 36 hours' notice, which they are allowed to do under the terms of the Stockholm Agreement, split into two pairs and were able, according to Air Vice Marshal Michael Stear, to see our troops 'just as they found us'. They were given all the usual facilities of a four-wheel drive vehicle and radio communications equipment, which are also provided for NATO observers at Warsaw Pact exercises.

Under normal circumstances inspectors would usually only be sent to watch manoeuvres involving more than 13,000 men. Exercise 'Drake's Drum' only involved some 5,000, most of them Territorials or members of the Home Service Force. Simulating Spetsnaz were numbers 21 and 23 SAS Regiments (TA). The Russians also sent an inspection team to observe exercise 'Bonnie Dundee' at the end of the month. This only involved some 4,400 men but was similarly designed to test the effectiveness of Scottish defences at such critical installations as the Faslane nuclear submarine base against Spetsnaz teams. In this instance, members of the Special Boat Squadron played the role of the saboteurs.

October 1988 produced some other, apparently unrelated, episodes. In two successive issues on the 2nd and 9th of the month *The Sunday Times* reported on the curious coincidence of deaths and disappearances amongst British scientists and technicians involved in defence related work since 1982, but particularly over the last couple of years. The Pentagon, they said, has asked for an investigation.

We are still waiting for an enquiry. But this was one aspect of what we feel is almost certainly Spetsnaz activity in the West which we had already been looking into for some time, and as far as we are concerned the problem is greater, the number of scientists involved larger, than anyone else is yet admitting.

Then the House of Lords threw out the Home Office injunction against the publication in England of Peter Wright's book *Spycatcher*, an injunction which cost over £1 million but which was doomed to failure from day one in any case because anyone – such as ourselves – who had a vested interest in reading it could easily obtain a copy from abroad. Peter Wright says nothing about Spetsnaz, though, which is rather strange in a book which claims to make so many other revelations. Nor does he mention the Royal Navy's Commander Lionel 'Buster' Crabb, the files on whose supposed death in 1956 will not be released until the next century. We have our own evidence on that mysterious case though, and the link with Spetsnaz which we have established (Chapter 4).

A conference of British and American security chiefs met at Ditchley Park in Oxfordshire following the *Spycatcher* decision, to discuss whether British intelligence needed the same sort of 'housecleaning' exercise which swept through the Central Intelligence Agency in the wake of the Watergate scandal, and the establishment of a 'watchdog' committee. This is said to have been vetoed by Prime Minister Margaret Thatcher, who presumably knows more than the journalists who commented on the conference. As the Americans have found, a clandestine organization, whether classed as 'security' or 'intelligence', cannot function efficiently in the limelight. Russians learnt his lesson in their cradles.

Autumn in England is the season of major party political conferences, some of the issues being confused in 1988 by the fact that they coincided with the run-up to the American presidential elections. Two things happened of relevance to this book, however. Mr Ron Todd threw down a gauntlet to Labour leader Neil Kinnock by putting his three million trades union block vote behind unilateral nuclear disarmament – the issue on which the Labour Party lost the last General Election. And hardline Communist Ken Gill[3] assumed the leadership of the Manufacturing Science Finance Union, Britain's fifth largest, when the much respected moderate, Clive Jenkins, took early retirement for personal reasons. A combination of the policies of Messrs Todd, Gill and other extremists such as the miners' leader, Arthur Scargill, could deliver the United Kingdom into Moscow's hands without a shot being fired if the British electorate permits it.

The infiltration and support of extreme left-wing organizations throughout the West has been a KGB speciality for decades, but in Spetsnaz we believe the USSR has recently found another tool equally skilled and ruthless. So who are they, really, these Moscow 'supermen'?

Well, 'supermen' is one thing they are not. Trained, skilled and motivated to the highest possible levels, yes. Qualified parachutists, divers, explosives experts, and, where necessary, assassins, yes. Possessing an unusually high officer/NCO ratio to enlisted men, yes. Backed by the largest military intelligence organization the world has ever seen, yes. Dedicated to the total overthrow of what we call 'democracy', yes. They will use any method that presents itself to reconnoitre their designated targets; to gain the technological information the GRU wants, to infiltrate themselves into Western life, as at Greenham Common (see Chapter 9); and to prop up organizations which aim to disrupt and ultimately demolish Western governments.

In this book we begin by examining the Spetsnaz role in time of war – but it should be understood that by this we mean 'hot' as opposed to 'cold' war, for despite de-Stalinization and all Mr Gorbachev's smiles, the Soviet Union has been involved in an ideological war against the West for decades; nor is the struggle yet over. In fact, it seems to be intensifying.

A fortnight before the Armenian earthquake disaster forced a postponement of Mr Gorbachev's visit to England to meet Mrs Thatcher, the *Sunday Express*' Political Editor, Anthony Smith, revealed that one item on the agenda was almost certain to be the worrying extent of KGB and GRU activity in the United Kingdom. 'Intelligence sources have revealed', he wrote on 27 November 1988, 'that the number of Russian agents has grown so rapidly since Mr Gorbachev came to power that Britain would be justified in expulsions on the sensational scale of 1971, when ninety spies were thrown out and another fifteen barred from re-entering.'

According to Mr Smith, D15 Director-General Patrick Graham has warned Mrs Thatcher that the KGB and GRU have 'stepped up all the old techniques of the Cold War – blackmail, subversion and attempted coercion of British nationals', all of which are issues already discussed later in this book. Moreover, Mr Smith said that D15 has specifically focused attention on those areas which we believe are the immediate targets of GRU/Spetsnaz attention:

'Their main quest is for military, technical and industrial know-how. Key targets are highly sensitive NATO-linked projects such as the US Stealth bomber, the Trident programme, Star Wars technology, and military-based laser and computer technology.' As will be seen in Chapter Eight, the last of these areas is currently the most disturbing.

In Chapter Three, therefore, we look at the structure of the KGB and the GRU and Spetsnaz's place within the overall framework of the Soviet armed forces. We show some of the means by which Spetsnaz teams are spying out the West and reconnoitring their potential targets. We look at the strange ways in which some of the top people connected with defence industries of prime interest to the GRU have died. And we discuss the global infrastructure of Communist subversion which exists to aid and abet Spetsnaz operatives whenever and wherever needed.

Our motivation for writing this book is simple. There is a grave threat to the fabric of a society in which we believe, a society which, by and large, has eliminated the cruder injustices and invasions of personal liberty; one which, in England at least, does not demand that each individual carry an identification card that the police can ask for at any time; one in which telephone bugging or mail interception demands the highest level of authorization; one in which torture or the use of drugs during interrogation is frowned upon[4]. We do not say that Western society, even in the most liberal of countries, is perfect. We do say that it is better than the society Moscow has never ceased trying to impose on the rest of the world, and that Spetsnaz is a direct threat to its existence about which precious little seems to be being done despite numerous pleas for enquiries.

Even if the results are never published, for security reasons, it would be nice to know that the authorities, somewhere, are taking action.

Mike Welham
Bruce Quarrie
January 1989

Notes Introduction

[1] The term 'Spetsnaz' is not used in this context within academic military circles despite its popular circularization because *Voyska Specialnoye Naznachenia* simply means 'special designation troops' and in Soviet military parlance can relate to arms of service other than elite special forces, including railway construction workers, for example.

[2] For the purposes of this narrative, the wording 'terrorist group(s)' is defined as an organization which uses, or seeks to use, violence as a means to a political end directed against the lawfully elected government of any country which possesses such a government (eg, the Provisional IRA in Northern Ireland). 'Freedom fighter(s)' denotes any similar organization which uses, or seeks to use,

violence as a means to a political end directed against an illegally imposed government or administration not generally acceptable to the majority of that country's population (eg, the Mujaheddin in Afghanistan). When you get to parts of Africa or South America, for example, though, the differentiation is often marginal at best. We have sought to avoid political bias wherever possible but this book is about Communist infiltration of the West and, to a lesser extent, what is generally referred to as the 'Third World', and we offer no apologies for any offence we cause to anyone who believes that the world would be better off run from Moscow.

[3] Gill was actually expelled from the Communist Party of Great Britain (CPGB) in 1985 because of his extreme attitudes, and according to *The Sunday Times* (16 October 1988), which described him as a 'Stalinist', he and his followers are known by other Communists 'as "tankies" for [their] undeviating pro-Moscow stance'.

[4] We accept that these techniques are both used by Western security agencies on occasion, as organizations such as Amnesty International and the European Court of Human Rights have both established over the years. But the average Englishman or American does not fear for his liberty, health or sanity in the same way as does someone who can be consigned without open trial or right of appeal to a Gulag or 'psychiatric hospital'.

Chapter One
Behind enemy lines

We rose and turned to face the distant space below us. Our hands gripped the parachute control rings. The green light flashed on. 'We're off!'

Something caught at my breath. I was unable to shut my eyes even though I wanted to. There was a slight jerk at the collar of my camouflage smock – the tiny stabilizing parachute turned me over head upwards. Rate of fall: 35 metres a second. I started counting. The main parachute should open on 'five'. 'Seven ... eight ... nine ...' Anxiety distorts your time sense. A click behind my back. An invisible hand pulled at me and my body rolled into a ball. There was a sharp 'crack', a hard jerk, something burned my left cheek ... then silence.

The grey and yellow canopy obscured half the sky. Above me I knew would be Major Vassilly Fedorovich Yackmenev, below me and a little ahead Major Anatoli Ivanovich Soldatenko. The ground was now only 500 metres below. I could see a forest with a few clearings and a stream. One hundred metres. The wind had turned the parachute and I was descending backwards. Looking desperately over my shoulder I could see a small clearing containing two massive tree stumps. I pulled at the rear shrouds of the parachute harness with all my strength. I wanted to turn to face those damned tree stumps. Too late! Maybe not, though. The stumps disappeared beneath my legs.

Something slammed me below the belt. A headstand, a somersault over a moss-covered hummock and I was being dragged towards the edge of the clearing. Major Soldatenko helped collapse the 'chute and get rid of the harness. We ran into the trees, leaving the space clear for the men following.

They crashed into the long grass or slid down from the treetops. 'Secure your weapons! Check your haversacks!' The rest of the snatch team quickly complied – Lieutenant Gennady Glotov and Sergeants Nikolai Vashurkin and Aleksei Korchagin.

The loaf of white bread and two hefty tins of stewed meat and some fish had to be tucked away wherever they would fit because we were fully laden down. Poncho, camouflage suit, spare footcloths[1], mess tin, spoon, a small net, fishing hooks and line, matches, a wire saw, packets of explosive, ammunition, a torch and the first aid kit including water purifying tablets all had to go in the haversacks. A flask of water, folding spade, a small axe and an automatic pistol were strapped to our belts. Our armament consisted of two silenced AKM assault rifles[2], a machine-gun[3], two RPG-7 portable anti-tank rockets[4], magnetic and other mines, detonators and flares. We also had two radio sets and spare batteries.

We disappeared into the forest like wraiths. The air was stuffy and humid. Mosquitoes whined and dry twigs cracked softly underfoot. We had fifty kilometres to cover in fifteen hours ...

* * *

The devil himself could not have found our hiding place next day. Each of us chose our own position – a fallen tree, an uprooted tree stump, a thick alder grove, a willow thicket, a sedge. My feet ached with cramp, their soles swollen and burning. I felt I lacked the strength to ever move again. Ahead of us lay a large lake with a village on the far side. We could see some boys playing with a boat and women washing linen and scouring pans. Nothing disturbed the idyllic scene. Even the birds soon got used to our presence and settled back to chattering and warbling between themselves. All the same, we dared not approach the lake but drank from a stream within the cover of the woods, after first dropping sterilizing tablets into our mess tins. It tasted like stale mineral water.

Three o'clock in the morning. After resting throughout the daylight we moved out under cover of darkness, and finally came to the edge of the woods. A sandy cart track led us past a small village, its inhabitants fast asleep. The dim light of the false dawn found us moving stealthily along the bottom of an overgrown gully in the direction of the sentry, who was quietly whistling to himself. The lad was bored and inattentive. When he fell silent, we held our breath.

A twig cracked loudly on the other side of the road: Korchagin. The sentry turned towards the sound and began to raise his rifle. As if propelled by a catapult, Glotov sprang from behind a bush. Vashurkin hurled himself at the guard's legs. One huge hairy hand wrapped itself around his mouth and pulled his head back, the other seized his throat. Within seconds he was gagged.

Thoroughly trussed up, the lad was breathing heavily and trembling, looking glassily up at us as though we were creatures from another world. We lifted him on to Korchagin's back and carried him like a dummy into the bushes. Here, Glotov unfolded the map and shone his torch on it while Korchagin aimed his own torch – and his automatic pistol – at the face of the prisoner.

'Who are you? What's the number of your unit? What is the surname and rank of your commanding officer? Where is your HQ situated? Where is the missile battery? Show it to us on the map. Who is guarding it at this moment? When are you supposed to be relieved? In fifteen minutes? You said the Major was with you? Where is he now? Asleep? In the truck? Oh, underneath it. How far is it to the battery?'

I was watching the lad closely. Information was pouring from him like water from a tap. Glotov seemed to be reading my thoughts. According to the rules of the exercise, the 'prisoner' should play the game. If you were captured, your part had come to an end and you had to answer all the 'enemy' questions[5].

So, we had fifteen minutes. We covered the 400 metres to the half-track truck parked at the edge of the village in one swift movement. Four men leapt like cats into the cab and grabbed the driver, who fought back like a man possessed, and pinned him to the ground while Glotov and I looked for the Major. He was stretched out blissfully under the vehicle in a sleeping bag. 'Get up! You are under arrest!' The Major woke up, raised his hands, then quickly rolled on to his stomach to reach his trouser belt. Glotov kicked it away. 'I said: "Get up!"'

* * *

The raid on the battery was a success[6]. So far we had been lucky, but now the 'enemy' would be alerted to our presence in the vicinity. Afterwards, we returned to 'our' wood to hide and cook our first hot meal for two days – warmed up stew and hot, refreshing tea.

Six minutes past midnight. The stars had vanished and the

forest was hushed. The first drops of rain began to fall and we covered our weapons. Then there was a brilliant flash followed by an ear-splitting clap of thunder. Within minutes we were soaked. The flashes of lightning turned the forest into a place of wonder – and danger. We dashed from one tree to another expecting a bolt of lightning to incinerate us at any moment. Our boots filled with water, we huddled in whatever meagre shelter we could find and roundly cursed the universal 'them' for not having invented a waterproof tobacco.

The rain eased up at around three in the morning, hastened away by a warm breeze. The forest began to rustle, whisper and creak. The birds were still silent as we moved out. Then the man on point gave the cut-off signal to stop. He had seen or heard something. Glotov eased forward to find out what. Someone or something was watching us. Deer, perhaps? No! A sudden burst of automatic weapons' fire from *behind* us. We threw ourselves to the ground. More fire from right and left. Ambush!

Sticking to our training, we did not return fire, which would have confirmed our presence, but melted into the wood, heading for the stream where we could hopefully lose our pursuers. A few kilometres along its sandy bottom would definitely cover our traces. A little more wetness would not hurt us! Carrying our weapons and explosives head high to stop *them* getting wet soon became a strain, though. We could not drink for fear of cramps, only rinse our mouths out. At last a halt was called, but we could not risk a fire to dry our sodden clothing. A seemingly abandoned haystack provided welcome warmth and shelter, and we slept through the day again. In the evening we tried the radio direction finder and detected enemy signals traffic from a village some ten kilometres away. This was roughly where earlier aerial reconnaissance on which we had been briefed had spotted signs of caterpillar tracks in the ground. There was no reason for tanks to be there. Missile carriers or artillery then? We had to find out.

We reached the area the transmissions had come from shortly after eleven o'clock that night and planned to rest until after midnight before making our move. The enemy transmitter was still pouring out a stream of incomprehensible numbers – were they on to us?

In the village all was quiet and peaceful. We crept through garden allotments to avoid detection, but could see the imprint of caterpillar tracks on the road. These led us to a barrier with an 'out of bounds' notice. Not to us, though! The starlight revealed barbed wire, watchtowers and several long, low mounds in the ground. Ammunition dumps of some sort! And well camouflaged against aerial detection. 'Down to work, boys.'

The AKM assault rifle's bayonet and scabbard can be fixed together in such a way as to form an effective wire cutter, so the first barrier was no problem. Three men with blasting charges slid through the gaps while the rest of us took aim at the watchtowers, just in case. The sappers disappeared into the darkness. A nervewracking forty minutes passed before they returned. 'OK,' said Glotov, 'fall back now.' On the nearest watchtower a floorboard creaked and we huddled silently against the earth. No sign of an alarm, though, so we wormed our way on elbows and knees until we were nearly half a kilometre away. Our job had been done. The explosive charges our sappers had laid would be exploded by radio signal from our distant headquarters at the appropriate time.

* * *

We had been in the field for 96 hours now. Towards morning on the fifth day our faithful woods gave way to a hard-surfaced highway which we had to cross. Scouts detected two enemy vehicles, one with a transmitter aerial. Damn! Further down the road were two armoured personnel carriers which must have carried at least twenty men. Even worse, there was a helicopter hidden in a clearing. To compound our problems, neither radio was working, so we could not communicate our predicament to headquarters[7]. We slipped back into the woods, moving several kilometres to avoid detection. That evening, we ate the last of our rations. Our packs were lighter, but from now on we would have to forage unless we could cross the highway to the rendezvous where we were supposed to receive an air drop of supplies the following night.

Glotov finally managed to get one of the radios working again, or perhaps it had dried out of its own accord. He asked for instructions. 'Act according to circumstances.' Very helpful. 'Will there be presents [supplies] tomorrow?' 'We cannot guarantee it. Listen out from 23:40 to midnight. Try to contact us again in three days' time. We wish you success.' Thanks for nothing!

Morning brought low clouds and a steady, dispiriting

drizzle. We had left our stream behind so had to drink tasteless rainwater as it dripped from our ponchos. The irrepressible Glotov designed some exercises to keep us alert – practising crossing a minefield. Then we did some gymnastics. Two of us would throw a third man into the air where he had to somersault and land a knife in a target before his feet touched the ground again. We tried the same thing using our spades, which are balanced so that they can also be used as weapons. After all this, without having had anything to eat, Glotov sent four of us to reconnoitre the nearest village. The others would have another look at the highway. So much for making our supply drop.

If we thought Glotov was a sadist, we soon found he was a damned good soldier too. The village was a trap! Korchagin and I watched, sitting in stinging nettles in an orchard. An electric generator was running in a farm pigsty. When it was turned off, we saw the farm women returning home but also heard someone left inside testing his radio. The enemy was trying to drive us into a 'sack', pursuers behind and an ambush in front, like herding sheep into a pen. We slipped away, unnoticed. The other party had no luck, either. The highway was being patrolled for two kilometres each side of the roadblock. Fortunately our excursion to the farm had produced some food for our rumbling stomachs – even if only apples, cucumbers and carrots.

* * *

The seventh day of the exercise brought us near an airfield which Glotov marked on his map, now soggy and muddy but filled with cryptic symbols showing the enemy positions we had noted as well as such invaluable things for follow-up teams as to where fish, berries or mushrooms could be found. In order to get to the airfield, though, we first had to swim a large lake. To do this, we stuffed our ponchos with grass and bracken, then put our weapons, torches and everything else which would suffer from getting wet into them and tied them into firm bundles. These we pushed ahead of us while we swam. Glotov, of course, went first, but after only a few minutes in the warm water beneath the dark sky we had lost all sense of direction and reckoned he must have too. We felt as though we had been swimming in circles for hours when, suddenly, we could feel bottom again and swished quietly through the reeds to the opposite shore. Some ducks were disturbed by our passage and we stood rooted to the spot in case they alerted someone. Nothing. The swim had made us all hungry again but all we could find was a few withered nuts with tiny milky kernels. Twigs cracked underfoot as we staggered ashore. 'Why are you crashing around like elephants! Be quiet!' Screw you too, Lieutenant.

Another haystack gave us cover that day. We could hear military traffic on a nearby road and see aircraft on obvious landing approaches. In the evening we found a stream and the water gave our bellies some satisfaction, then we hid in a decrepit barn, its rotten floorboards stinking with damp and other things better not to mention. Mosquitoes were a constant plague. Later, we heard aircraft approaching and Glotov climbed to the upper floor to get a better look. The aircraft were flying slowly towards the town whose lights lit the distant horizon. The Lieutenant watched them through his binoculars. Low over the forest domes were opening. Parachutes! Could this be our supply drop at long last, or was it enemy reinforcements?

By next morning, our eighth day in the field, we knew the worst. The enemy was still trying to box us in, and we knew our pursuers from the earlier ambush could not be far behind. The town, our next objective, was still fifteen kilometres away, and there was too much traffic for us to attempt crossing the highway. To add to our hunger and general unshaven misery, we were forced to evade capture by stumbling through a peat bog. Glotov split us into two parties to try to cross the road. 'We'll rendezvous at the bend in the stream at 23:00 hours,' he said, 'Synchronize watches. It's now 21:43.'

Crawling through the sedge, Glotov and I, together with two others, reached the road unobserved at a point where a culvert ran underneath an embankment. A twig snapped, something tinkled and snorted. A cow! There had to be a farmhouse nearby. We crawled along the brook towards the pipe. A woman walked past, apparently calling for one of her children. I don't know how she avoided seeing us. Then a lorry passed, moving quickly and spraying us with gravel. Not much further now! Someone on the embankment threw a cigarette into the brook just in front of our noses. A sentry? An approaching car and motor cycle gave us covering noise and we darted for the narrow mouth of the pipe. The air was stuffy and we hurried to the other side of the road. Suddenly, there was the distant sound of automatic fire. Then another burst. We looked at each other anxiously.

23:00 hours. No sign of our comrades. They had been 'killed' or captured. Glotov got through to HQ on the radio and reported our situation. We held our breath as he listened through the headphones. His face was inscrutable as he took them off and thoughtfully rubbed his stubbly chin. 'Well ...' he said, leaving us in a moment's further suspense before his face creased in a wide grin, 'in two hours' time there will be an aircraft in square 40. They will drop us an engineer expert in blasting operations and two more men in plain clothes.' There was obviously more to come but the Lieutenant kept the best for last. 'Have you all got your mess tins still? They promise us a good supper and a whole 24 hours' rest. Let's go!'

The exercise continued for another twenty days.

Notes Chapter One

[1] Soviet soldiers traditionally wrapped their feet in cloths, and it is only very recently that they have started being issued with socks.

[2] The AKM in 7.62 mm calibre was for many years the successor to the venerable AK-47 so widely used by 'freedom fighters' around the world. Although the AKM remains in widespread use, it has largely been replaced in the Soviet front line over recent years by the 5.45 mm calibre AK-74 which fires hollow point 'dum-dum' rounds even though they are outlawed internationally. The AKM weighs 3.98 kg and has a curved thirty-round box magazine. It has a muzzle velocity of 710 m/sec and a cyclic rate of fire of 600 rounds per minute.

[3] Probably a 7.62 mm RPK, which is basically an AKM with a longer barrel and bipod mount able to fire 75-round drum or 30- or 40-round box magazines with a slightly higher muzzle velocity and rate of fire (732 m/sec and 660 rpm). The heavier PK machine-gun is unlikely to be used by infiltration squads.

[4] The RPG-7 is a bazooka-style weapon firing an over-calibre 85 mm hollow charge projectile from a 40 mm diameter launch tube. It has an effective range of some 500 m and its 2.25 kg warhead gives armour penetration of 320 mm.

[5] As do the SAS and SBS among other elite special forces, Spetsnaz troops conduct exercises against each other in which the rules are often quite different. Escape and evasion techniques are taken very

seriously indeed, and in the SAS and SBS a man can be RTU'd (returned to unit) if he breaks under interrogation and gives away anything more than the statutory 'name, rank and number'. It is logical to assume that Spetsnaz use the same methods to teach their members how to hold out under interrogation.

[6] There are frustrating gaps in the original narrative.

[7] One of the reasons the GRU is so anxious to obtain Western technology is because Soviet electronic equipment is notoriously unreliable in the field, though this is nothing new! In this instance, the thunderstorm probably played a major role.

Chapter Two
Voyska Spezialnoye Naznachenia

Chapter One is a colloquially translated factual account[1] of one Evgeny Meyatser's experiences during part of a month-long Spetsnaz exercise 'behind enemy lines'. What it so graphically illustrates is the part Spetsnaz troops are expected to play in time of conventional war or during the build-up period before a nuclear exchange. Their tasks are reconnaissance, sabotage, subversion – and murder. They are tough, determined, ruthless, highly trained and motivated and skilled in all forms of armed and unarmed combat. In this they are not alone, but only recently has sufficient information come to light to accord them the same global recognition already given to the American Green Berets, SEALs and Operational Detachment Delta or the British Special Air Service Regiment and Special Boat Squadron. These Western forces have received considerable publicity – much to their own chagrin, for secrecy is one of their principal weapons – in such events as the Iranian Embassy siege in London, the attempted rescue of American hostages in Tehran, and the campaigns in the Falklands and Grenada. Until the Soviet invasion of Afghanistan, however, practically no-one in the West had heard the name 'Spetsnaz', and even today many of the ramifications of this clandestine force are unknown outside higher Soviet military and intelligence circles.

Like all other modern special forces, the Spetsnaz can date their origins back to the Second World War. When Nazi

24

Germany invaded the Soviet Union on 22 June 1941, it was only a matter of days before small groups of partisans began emerging to strike at the enemy's rear areas. Partly the partisan units were composed of civilians with intimate knowledge of their own localities and partly of army personnel who had evaded capture after becoming separated from their units. Their targets were vehicle convoys, isolated outposts, telephone and railway lines, ammunition and petrol dumps and other targets of opportunity. To begin with these groups operated in virtual isolation from each other with little or no co-ordination but their activities soon came to the attention of Moscow where the Central Committee of the Communist Party created the Central Staff of the Partisan Movement which was headed by Major-General Pavel Sudoplatov. This not only co-ordinated the activities of the hundreds of independent groups but assigned them targets and supplied them with weapons, explosives and radio operators just as the British Strategic Operations Executive (SOE) and, later, American Office of Strategic Services (OSS) helped and co-ordinated the various resistance groups in occupied Europe.

As the war progressed the partisan forces in western Russia grew to an enormous size and were organized into entire brigades with a military infrastructure, striking and then disappearing back into the trackless wastes of Russia's many huge forests and marshes where it took a foolhardy German to follow. The men parachuted in to assist and direct the partisan effort were mainly from the Soviet Airborne Forces, and Spetsnaz has subsequently retained close links with the regular airborne units from whom most of its personnel are recruited, just as the Parachute Regiment provides the majority of men for the SAS. The partisan efforts cannot be quantified but they resulted in the Germans having to create several entire divisions of security troops to try and contain their activities, troops who would have been more profitably deployed in the front line.

After the war had been won there was a general reorganization throughout the Red Army and this included what had become known as the *voyska spezialnoye naznachenia*, or special purpose troops, generally abbreviated to Spetsnaz although it is only in recent years that the general public in the West has learned of their existence. Even within the Soviet armed forces, their existence is generally kept secret and, like the men of the SAS and other elite forces, Spetsnaz troops generally wear the standard uniforms of either Russian airborne or naval infantry. (The only way of telling them apart lies in the *absence* of Guards insignia on their berets and tunic patches. They also have their own peculiar camouflage smocks with hoods shown in some of the photographs.) In creating Spetsnaz a further influence was the shock brigades (*udarnaya brigada*) also formed during the war from hand-picked volunteers of fanatical conviction who would rather die than surrender (a characteristic inherited by the Spetsnaz). Leonid Brezhnev commanded such a brigade at one point.[2]

The prime mover in the creation of today's Spetsnaz was General Viktor Kondratevich Kharchenko, an engineering officer on the General Staff with an inquiring scientific mind. He led the way in pioneering a greater degree of technical training to give the *voyska spezialnoye naznachenia* a better understanding of the tools with which they would have to work, from weapons and explosives to electronic equipment, and was forceful in insisting that the special forces should have priority access to the latest 'kit'.[3]

The Soviet Union is openly committed to the destruction of capitalism and the establishment worldwide of its own brand of communism. To this end it will deploy any suitable military or political tool, and one of the most valuable of these today is Spetsnaz. This is particularly true in the current period of *glasnost*, for the relaxation of East-West tensions over the last year or two has seen an intensification of Soviet clandestine activities – infiltration and espionage. Spetsnaz forces are playing a vital part in this throughout not just Europe but also in the vulnerable parts of the Third World. Some of the more ominous aspects of this are discussed in later chapters, but to begin with it is necessary to see the Spetsnaz role in the purely military context.

Spetsnaz teams operate in small units of four to a dozen men deep behind enemy lines as reconnaissance and sabotage units. They would also spearhead any conventional invasion of western Europe, being dropped by parachute or landed from submarines to seize key objectives in front of the main forces. The primary targets for Spetsnaz teams would be as follows. The most important of all are nuclear missiles. Before the Reagan-Gorbachev agreement, these would have included both Pershing and Ground-Launched Cruise Missile (GLCM)

sites but with the gradual removal of these, Spetsnaz teams
will be concentrating on the highly mobile Lance tactical
battlefield missiles deployed by American, British and West
German forces. If a Spetsnaz team observed such a missile
being readied for launch, its personnel would make a last
ditch attempt to destroy it with smallarms fire. Other nuclear
targets for these strike teams would include airfields housing
aircraft carrying nuclear bombs or missiles. Surface-to-air
(SAM) missile batteries such as Rapier guarding such bases
against air attack would be additional priority targets.
Nuclear submarines and warships carrying Sea-Launched
Cruise Missiles (SLCMs) would be other obvious objectives.
Spetsnaz infiltration of western European airfields, ports and
military depots by road and by sea to determine such targets
and allow team leaders to reconnoitre possible approaches
and obstacles *is already happening* and has been for some
time.

The second most important objective would be the
disruption at all levels of NATO political, strategic and
tactical Command, Control, Communications and Intelligence
(C³I) installations. This would involve sabotaging major links
in the chain, such as the Government Communications
Headquarters (GCHQ) at Cheltenham, the American
National Security Agency's (NSA's) principal signals intelligence establishment in Europe at Chicksands, in Bed-
fordshire, and other intelligence and early warning
establishments at Brawdy, Edzell, Fylingdales and Menwith
Hill. At a lower level, corps, division, and on occasion even
brigade, regimental and battalion command and communications vehicles would also be targets. Military and political
leaders would be specifically targetted for assassination.
Civilian telephone exchanges and radio and television
broadcasting stations would be attacked to add to the general
confusion, as would electronics, computer and defence-related
industrial plants. Portable anti-tank missiles would be
extremely useful in destroying radio and radar antennae [4]
from a distance and one of the reasons the Soviet Union
supplies such large quantities of these to terrorist organizations is so that in time of war Spetsnaz teams will find
readily accessible stocks of weapons already established in
enemy territory.

At a tactical level, Spetsnaz teams would spearhead attacks
on Western military garrisons and fuel dumps, and if

necessary secure the dropping zones and landing beaches they would be reconnoitring for follow-up parachute and seaborne forces, as well as key bridges, canal lock gates and the like. The interrogation of prisoners would be a further important task, all part of their general reconnaissance duties. The successful seizure of objectives and any intelligence information gathered would be reported by each team back to its Brigade headquarters using portable R-350M or even more recent radios capable of transmitting high speed 'squeezed' messages in code over a range greater than 1,000 km.

That intelligence gathering in rather more than the normal sense of 'reconnaissance' is seen by the Soviet Union as a Spetsnaz function even more important than sabotage and disruption is clear from the fact that the whole apparatus falls under the command of military intelligence, the GRU (*Glavnoe Razvedyvatelnoe Upravlenie*, or Main Intelligence Directorate.) The aims and organization of the GRU, and its relationship to the KGB, are discussed in the next chapter.

Total strength of the Spetsnaz forces today is variously estimated at between 15,000 and 30,000 men, and even if the lower figure is the more accurate (as seems likely) it makes Spetsnaz the largest 'elite' force trained in both overt and covert behind-the-lines warfare in the world. Not surprisingly, the Soviet Union refuses to acknowledge publicly the existence of Spetsnaz other than through oblique means. Two paragraphs in the *Soviet Military Encyclopaedia* are illuminating. The first discusses 'troops of special designation' and refers only to the special forces of America, Britain, France, Israel and Japan, leaving the unwary reader with the impression that the Soviet Union itself has no such units. This entry describes 'troops of special designation' as 'special units and sub-units in the armed forces in an array of capitalist states, designated for reconnaissance-sabotage and terrorist activities, the organization of rebellious activity and armed attacks, the directing of psychological war, propaganda and other subversive activity'. We have nothing to argue with here. The SAS would certainly agree that such activities fall within their own overall brief.

A more recent edition of the same book[5] describes 'special reconnaissance' (*spezialnaya razvedka*) as 'Reconnaissance carried out to subvert the political, economic and military potential and morale of a probable or actual enemy. The primary missions of special reconnaissance are: acquiring intelligence on major economic and military installations and either destroying them or putting them out of action; organizing sabotage and acts of subversion; carrying out punitive operations against rebels; conducting propaganda; forming and training insurgent detachments, etc. Special reconnaissance is ... conducted by the forces of covert intelligence and special purpose troops.'

We have nothing to argue with here either. However, in describing the West's special forces in this way, the Encyclopaedia is also giving a thumbnail sketch of Spetsnaz. Take it item by item.

'... subvert the economic and military potential and morale of a probable or actual enemy ...' Strikes and protest demonstrations achieve two of these objectives. The military is, fortunately, rarely affected in any serious way by either. The military does, though, rely on budgets which have to be approved by governments supposedly responsible to their electorates and therefore susceptible to the voters' whimsical changes of attitude. Subversion has traditionally been a KGB function, but increasingly over recent years Spetsnaz have been more and more involved.

'... acquiring intelligence on major economic and military installations and either destroying them or putting them out of action ...' There have been enough spy disclosures in recent years to show that the Soviet Union is very active in this field. The GRU is particularly concerned with the acquisition of scientific and technical knowledge and uses Spetsnaz as a peacetime intelligence-gathering tool, as will be seen. And what better way to put economic and military installations out of action than by killing key figures working in the front line of research?

'... organizing sabotage and acts of subversion ...' The PLO and other terrorist groups, particularly Libyan, could not function at a quarter of their efficiency without Soviet backing. Even the IRA – especially since President Reagan clamped down on the export of funds from American sympathisers (NORAID) – relies largely on the Warsaw Pact for arms and explosives. Although Communists and Catholics make uneasy bedfellows, a terrorist group will accept help from any source, and despite the fact that the ultimate aims of the KGB and GRU are not the same as those of the IRA extremists, Soviet intelligence will assist any group causing disruption in a Western country – particularly one which is a member of NATO.

'... carrying out punitive operations against rebels ...' From Moscow's point of view, a 'rebel' is anyone who opposes or otherwise stands in the way of the Kremlin's ultimate aims. The deaths of tens of thousands of people in Afghanistan and other countries (including Ireland and the UK) where the Soviet Union directly or indirectly aids and abets terrorist organizations come under this category.

'... conducting propaganda ...' Although not normally a Spetsnaz function any more than it is one of the SAS or SBS, Spetsnaz operatives alongside KGB and GRU agents would certainly assist when called upon so long as these tasks did not interfere with a more serious mission. Many left-wing magazines, newspapers and broadsheets could not survive through subscriptions and advertising alone. And many hardline trades unions could not continue all their activities without extra 'whitewashed' funding, much of which comes from Moscow.

'... forming and training insurgent detachments ...' A huge part of Eastern Bloc effort is devoted to this throughout the world. Spetsnaz instructors are particularly highly valued. The following table[6] showing Soviet, Cuban and East German involvement in a number of critical countries around the world probably represents only the tip of an iceberg. Figures are true but approximate for the mid-1980s because, obviously, precise numbers of 'military advisors' and other supporting personnel fluctuate quite rapidly. There are undoubtedly other omissions where no data is available.

Afghanistan gave the western world its first real picture of Spetsnaz in action, although earlier involvements have subsequently come to light. Many others must similarly remain unrevealed. In the late 1960s and early 1970s, during the peak period of US involvement in Vietnam, Spetsnaz teams were infiltrated to test operational methods and techniques as well as new equipment, such as the SVD sniper rifle, also known as the Dragunov. (This is basically an AK-47 but with a longer barrel giving an accurate range of 800-1,000 m. It fires a longer and more powerful cartridge than in the assault rifle but only has a ten-round magazine. Its telescopic sight acts as an accurate rangefinder and passive infra-red night sights can also be fitted.) Success in Vietnam led the SVD to be widely used in Afghanistan.

Country of involvement	Numbers of 'advisors' involved		
	Soviet	Cuban	East German
Afghanistan*	120,000	100	
Algeria	8,500	170	250
Angola	700	18,000	450
Congo	850	950	15
Cuba	12,000		
Ethiopia	2,400	9,000	550
Guinea	375	280	125
India	1,550		
Iraq	8,000	2,200	160
Libya	2,300	3,000	
Madagascar	370	55	
Mali	635		20
Mozambique	500	1,000	100
Nicaragua	50	3,200	
Peru	175	10	
Syria	4,000	5	210
Tanzania	300	95	15
Yemen, North	475		
Yemen, South	2,500	800	325

* At peak, before Soviet withdrawal commenced in 1988.

In 1968 Spetsnaz troops spearheaded the Soviet takeover of Czechoslovakia. A group attached to the 103rd Guards Airborne Division flew into Prague first, feigning engine trouble to gain landing clearance. Leaping from their aircraft, they seized guard posts and took over the control tower so as to bring in the airborne division. Officers from this team were also responsible for arresting Alexandr Dubjek and emplaning him for Moscow, as well as seizing key points in the city until they could be relieved by regular troops.

It was also a Spetsnaz hit team which spearheaded the invasion of Afghanistan in December 1979. A Company led by Colonel Byeronov a KGB officer, whose more normal job was running the KGB terrorist training school, attacked President Hazifullah Amin's palace on the outskirts of Kabul. The men had begun landing at Kabul airport on regular Aeroflot flights, dressed in civilian clothing, on 24 December. On Christmas Day, they locked up senior Afghan officers who had unwittingly attended a reception at the Soviet Embassy.

The following day, Boxing Day, dressed now in Afghan Army uniforms, they secured the airport and its approaches in a virtual replay of the Prague operation. They then moved in on the palace. Byeronov's orders were explicit. 'The secret of our action must be rigorously protected. Do not let any person leave the palace alive.' To Byeronov's surprise, Amin's bodyguard fought back with such skill and aggression that he had to call up a second Company in support. The President and all except one of his guards were killed. So, ironically, was Byeronov, shot accidentally by one of his own men. The survivor, a Captain who, equally ironically, had been trained in the Soviet Union, later gave his account to the French newspaper *Le Figaro*[7]. He was quoted as saying 'the Spetsnaz used weapons equipped with silencers and shot down their adversaries like professional killers'.

'Professional killer' is an exact definition of *any* soldier, of course. What the Spetsnaz Companies demonstrated was a savagery and skill in weapons use which would not be encountered in a normal regular. This is one of the reasons why Spetsnaz is so dangerous.

Spetsnaz teams were subsequently operational throughout the Soviet occupation of Afghanistan. Typical tasks included long-range patrolling deep within Mujahideen territory on 'search and destroy' missions to wipe out guerrilla groups; 'disinformation' exercises such as the burning of mosques while disguised as guerrillas to try to throw discredit on the Mujahideen movement; and reconnoitring suitable sites into which stronger air mobile troops could be spotted by helicopter on commanding ground along convoy routes. The use of helicopters has become very much a Spetsnaz speciality, just as it is in the special forces of other countries, of course.

At the peak of their involvement in Afghanistan, Spetsnaz fielded seven Brigades, although not always at full strength (see below). One of their tasks was to co-operate with the *Khad*, the Afghan secret police, in trying to infiltrate the Mujahideen. That this was at least partially successful can be seen in the numbers of successful Soviet raids on guerrilla camps and villages. Reports state that on occasion up to thirty large helicopters[8] carrying Spetsnaz troops were involved in large-scale raids.

The Soviet Union used every method of decimation possible against the Afghans. Banned chemical agents were certainly

Spetsnaz troops blend almost invisibly into their surroundings.

Above A Spetsnaz soldier peers through the barbed wire surrounding a target.

Below Spetsnaz troops dressed in their distinctive camouflage suits descend a rocky defile.

Above Springing seemingly from nowhere, a Spetsnaz trooper fells a sentry by means of a rugby-style tackle during an exercise.

Below Installations such as GCHQ would be prime targets for Spetsnaz in the period immediately preceding open conflict.

Bottom Similarly, naval installations such as Devonport would certainly come under attack.

KGB-trained border guards on the East German frontier.

This border guard has crossed the frontier wall to peer into the West more closely.

deployed, while heavy air raids on villages were followed up by Spetsnaz interrogation teams who used torture and rape as standard in the efforts to extract information about Mujahideen bases and movements[9]. A particularly evil Spetsnaz 'calling card' designed specifically to terrorize came in the form of booby-trapped toys which would maim any child who picked one up. Even fake copies of the Koran were found to be filled with plastic explosive.

The following report, headed 'Non-conventional tactics', is reproduced by kind permission of *Military Technology* magazine[10] and is revealing about Spetsnaz methods.

'The Soviets are increasingly using non-conventional tactics [in Afghanistan]. Night ambushes are now standard procedure, and there have been several surprise attacks against the guerrilla camps. These attacks were usually carried out immediately before dawn, when the Mujahideen were praying, and it took a tremendous effort for the guerrillas to change their religious habits and leave some armed men on watch during the prayers (five times a day).

'Contrary to standard practices for Western special forces, the Spetsnaz do not operate in small teams[11]. There are no known examples of Spetsnaz missions involving less than fifty men and the standard operational group is at company level (120 men) ...

'The Soviets have considerably improved their counter-guerrilla tactics, and by fully exploiting the possibilities offered by helicopter landings they are now able, in many cases, to keep and maintain the initiative. The usual operational scheme calls for paratroops being simultaneously landed in several different places within an area known to harbour or support guerrillas: a large-scale "search and kill" operation is then carried out for two or three days, and even should the guerrillas be able to escape, the Communists burn the crops, blow up the villages, and abduct or kill all those suspected of supporting the resistance.'

The Soviet occupation of Afghanistan caused an immense refugee problem. Some 1.9 million people fled to Iran and 3.2 million to Pakistan. Spetsnaz teams would have infiltrated these groups and gathered a great deal of vital information about Mujahideen plans and deployments simply by keeping their ears open, without resort to overt methods. Moreover, once in Iran or Pakistan, the Spetsnaz teams have been free to indulge in acts of sabotage such as blowing up bridges, railway lines and electricity power supplies, and placing bombs in crowded markets, cinemas and even schools. The aim of this was partly to wear down the resistance of the refugees and partly to create internal pressure from local people to have the refugees returned to their own country.

In all, at least half a million people were killed during the Soviet occupation of Afghanistan, but whereas western peace movements are vociferous about CIA involvement in Nicaragua, for example, on this subject they have been remarkably subdued. We shall return to this subject in Chapter Nine.

* * *

The Spetsnaz Brigade has an operational strength of up to 1,300 men (although 6-800 is more usual) divided into three or four Battalions plus Headquarters and Signals Companies and an independent anti-VIP Company comprising seventy to eighty men. (The latter are the true assassins. Each man is fluent in at least one language other than Russian and they would normally operate individually or in small groups wearing civilian clothes. Their targets are western political, military and scientific leaders and Chapter 8 gives an indication of how active they may already be.) Each battalion contains three companies, the usual complement of which is generally accepted as being nine officers, eleven warrant officers and 95 other ranks. Spetsnaz formations are normally distributed throughout the Red Army as follows: one brigade plus one Intelligence company to each army front, total sixteen of each; one independent company to each army, total 41; and one long-range reconnaissance regiment (two battalions, or 7-800 men) to each theatre[12] Commander-in-Chief, total three. The last-named regiments are entirely composed of career soldiers as opposed to conscripts, as are the headquarters companies within each regiment or brigade. A further Spetsnaz brigade is also assigned to work with each of the armed forces of Czechoslovakia, East Germany, Hungary and Poland, and the East Germans have now raised their own Spetsnaz-style forces (see below). Additionally, there are Spetsnaz formations within each of the Soviet Navy's four fleets, and these are discussed in Chapter Four.

The most up-to-date listing of Spetsnaz deployments available to us (October 1988) from the IAP-Service[13] leaves some gaps but shows that certain regions are considered more critical than others. There are sixteen military districts in Russia, coinciding with the army fronts, and the deployment of Spetsnaz brigades is said to be as follows. Far East and Trans-Baikal regions, three; Siberian, Central Asian, Urals, Volga and North Caucasus districts, none; Turkestan and Trans-Caucasus, one apiece; Odessa, Moscow and Leningrad, two each; and one in the Baltic, Belorussian, Carpathian and Kiev regions, plus one in East Germany and one in Hungary. The 'missing' brigades are, or were, almost certainly in Afghanistan.

All military recruitment in the Soviet Union is conducted through these sixteen districts, the headquarters of which are as follows: Moscow, Leningrad, Kiev, Odessa, Lvov (Carpathian), Minsk (Belorussian), Riga (Baltic), Sverdlovsk (Ural), Kubyshev (Volga), Rostov (North Caucasus), Tbilsi (Trans-Caucasus), Tashkent (Turkestan), Alma Ata (Central Asia), Novosibirsk (Siberia), Chita (Trans-Baikal) and Khabarovsk (Far East). Many of the Spetsnaz troops active in Afghanistan were from the Turkestan district, where the language and local dialects are similar.

Spetsnaz recruits are carefully selected from the cream of each year's conscript intake, the GRU being given priority even over the strategic rocket, nuclear submarine and airborne forces. Every Soviet male is called up at the age of eighteen but even before this recruiting officers will have had their eyes on likely candidates. 'All rounders' are the boys most in demand, those who excel at school both academically and on the sports field. They also have to be members of the Communist youth organisation Komsomol, thus indicating political reliability. Membership of the DOSAAF[14] is regarded as an asset because it demonstrates a leaning towards the military way of thinking, but is not essential. Boys who do join DOSAAF have the opportunity to learn gliding, parachuting and scuba diving amongst other skills which will stand them in good stead in the armed forces. In Spetsnaz, preference is also given to boys from rural areas who will have a better knowledge and understanding of the countryside than those city-bred and will thus be better able to live off the land during deep penetration missions.

Each conscript has to serve for two years, turnover

averaging 1.7 million per year, after which he goes into the reserve. At any given point during peacetime, there are roughly 4.1 million men (conscripts and regulars) on the active list and some nine million in the reserves, excluding KGB border guards, etc (375,000), Ministry of the Interior troops (200,000 involved in internal security duties and guarding the Gulags) and construction troops (250,000). Most of these are in the 'teeth' formations – the eight airborne, 46 armoured and 119 motorized rifle divisions and thirteen airborne brigades which are kept up to between 50 and 75 per cent of their full strength. Other formations are normally kept at between a quarter and a third of their full establishment but mobilizing the reserves would bring the 'teeth' formations to full strength within a matter of days and the remainder within a few weeks. Only Spetsnaz and the 'quick reaction' airborne units are kept at full strength all the time.

Basic training is harsh and for many conscripts from the Soviet Union's far-flung provinces made harder because the only language allowed to be spoken is Russian. Initially it is the same for all conscripts, even those earmarked as having Spetsnaz potential, and lasts three months. After this, the best recruits are sent on a gruelling six-month NCO training course from which only one in five will graduate. These are the future Spetsnaz team leaders. Those who fail become ordinary Privates within Spetsnaz. but, having undergone the course, can take over in the field when necessary. All members of Spetsnaz, whether Army or Navy, are trained in high and low altitude and free fall parachute jumping[15]. They receive bonus pay for this which can double their salary, already at least fifty per cent greater than that of any other members of the armed forces (some sources put Spetsnaz pay even higher but it is difficult to rationalize this). The extra money is partly a reward for the extremely rigorous and often hazardous training, and partly an incentive to induce conscripts to 'go career'.

Spetsnaz recruits do not just have to learn normal soldiering skills – smallarms usage, fieldcraft, enemy equipment recognition, first aid, NBC[16] protection, etc – but a great deal more. Instruction in map reading, cross-country navigation, living off the land and constructing virtually invisible 'hides' is obviously vital for troops who will be expected to operate as far as a thousand kilometres behind enemy lines. For those who show the aptitude, extra languages are taught, English and German being the two most important. Extra weapons training in the use of NATO small arms parallels that in western special forces in using Warsaw Pact weaponry. The use of explosives is also vital for the sabotage mission, as well as handling acids and abrasives. A great deal of time is spent on unarmed combat and the use of silent killing devices – knives, the garotte, the trusty spade whose use as a weapon as well as a tool is taught throughout the Red Army and, for those selected to join the anti-VIP Companies, poisons. Signals, codes and ciphers, interrogation techniques and, equally importantly, techniques for resisting interrogation are also taught, and each Spetsnaz soldier is said to have to swear an oath to kill himself rather than divulge information to an enemy. Mountain and arctic warfare methods, including rock climbing, abseiling and skiing, are also learned.

Spetsnaz officers either come up from the ranks after completing their conscription period and choosing the armed forces as a career, or are recruited from other arms of service – particularly the airborne divisions, as already noted. But Spetsnaz has great need for specialists as well, and intelligence, signals and engineering officers in particular are often recruited. To many of these officers, the revelation of the mere existence of Spetsnaz often comes as a shock when they are first approached – after careful vetting, of course. Following induction and training, officers and senior NCOs will spend some considerable time familiarizing themselves with life in the West and reconnoitring potential target areas, either visiting European, Scandinavian and other countries as tourists, being given a cover posting to an embassy or consulate, or, as we shall see, posing as merchant seamen or lorry drivers.

Spetsnaz teams can, and obviously do, operate in isolation for prolonged periods of time in open countryside. In crowded western Europe, however, such a qualification is less necessary than on NATO's border flanks in Norway and Turkey, where the terrain and living conditions are comparatively harsh. In Europe, which is where Spetsnaz attentions are principally focused, Spetsnaz teams will probably have more limited, short term goals than they have to contend with in other parts of the world. They will be the harbingers of destruction, bringing panic and confusion before larger airborne and naval units are landed and the tanks begin to roll.

The Russian airborne forces are organized and equipped as

follows (naval infantry are discussed later). There are eight permanent divisions privileged with 'Guards' status, ten separate assault brigades and three independent 'air agile' brigades. According to IAP-Service again, at the time of writing there were parts of two divisions, the 103rd and 105th, plus one assault brigade in the process of being withdrawn from Afghanistan. The balance of the 105th Division was in Turkestan and the 103rd in Belorussia. Two assault brigades and two agile brigades are stationed in the Far East and one assault brigade in the Central Asian province, both flanking China. In the west, the 106th Division is stationed outside Moscow, the 76th and an assault brigade in Leningrad district, the 7th and 44th Divisions and an assault brigade in the Baltic province, the 98th Division and an assault brigade in Odessa and the 104th in Trans-Caucasus. The remaining two assault brigades are in the Carpathian province and East Germany.

Each division consists of circa 6,600 men with some 330-350 BMD mechanized infantry combat vehicles, 31-36 ASU-85 airborne assault guns and roughly sixty artillery pieces and mortars. The BMD (*Boyevaya Maschina Desantnaya*, or air-delivered combat vehicle) is a small fully-tracked armoured personnel carrier capable of carrying six infantrymen in addition to its crew of three. It is amphibious and armed either with a 73 mm smoothbore gun loaded from a forty-round automatic magazine or, in the BMD-81-1 variant, by a high velocity 30 mm cannon similar to that in the British Scimitar. A turretless command version with extra electronic gear is also produced. In addition to its gun armament, the BMD is fitted with a launch post for AT-3 'Sagger' anti-tank missiles or, more recently, for AT-5 'Spandrels'; three 7.62 mm machine-guns are also standard, giving the BMD considerable flexibility in taking on other vehicles up to main battle tanks, or enemy infantry. Weighing only nine tonnes, it can be dropped on a pallet by parachute, be driven on roads at up to 80 km/h or through water at 10 km/h, and has an estimated range of some 400 km.

The Soviet Union uses special pallets containing retro-rockets in their base to slow the descent rate of air-dropped vehicles and other heavy equipment. A weight is dangled 20 m below the pallet: when this makes contact with the ground, the rockets fire automatically, giving such a soft landing that the BMDs and other vehicles barely rock on their springs. One of these is the ASU-85 assault gun which, although now obsolescent (having been around since the 1960s), is still an important weapon in the airborne forces' armoury because, even though designated an 'assault gun', it is more properly speaking a tank destroyer. It is fully tracked with armour protection up to 40 mm thick and mounts a D-70 85 mm rifled gun in a limited traverse mounting in the front of the superstructure. This can fire armour-piercing high explosive (APHE) or high velocity armour-piercing (HVAP) rounds as well as ordinary high explosive fragmentation shells, and again forty rounds are carried. Unlike the BMD, the ASU-85 is not amphibious. It has a top speed of 44 km/h and a range of 260 km.

Other weapons unique to the airborne forces' inventory include the sixteen-barrel RPU-14 multiple rocket launcher and the old 82 mm mortar which is no longer used by other branches of the Red Army because of its lack of range and 'punch', but which is retained by the paras because of its low weight. The airborne troops can also call upon the whole gamut of other Soviet equipment, including the RPG-7 anti-tank rocket launcher and the more recent RPG-16 and -18, the latter being a direct copy of the American 66 mm LAW (Light Armour Weapon), a collapsible bazooka-style weapon which is thrown away once it has been fired. A new 85 mm anti-tank gun, believed to be a smoothbore but about which no details are yet available, and older 82 and 107 mm recoilless guns are also used by the airborne troops, alongside the 2S-3 self-propelled gun and M-1979 multiple rocket launcher.

For air defence the airborne troops are equipped with twin fast-firing 23 mm guns on lightweight wheeled trailers; the SA–9 'Gaskin' surface-to-air (SAM) missile, usually mounted in fours on BRDM-2 wheeled carrier vehicles; and the SA-7 'Grail' man-portable anti-aircraft missile developed from the American Redeye.

The airborne assault brigades each have approximately 3,000 men and are equipped with about fifty BMDs, while the 'agile' brigades are just 1,800 strong and do not appear to have any BMDs, although this situation may be changing.

* * *

Should it ever come, a major Soviet offensive in western Europe is unlikely to be in the form of an unannounced pre-emptive nuclear strike, for the Soviet government regardless of whoever currently holds the reins of power knows that this would provoke untenable retaliation. Moreover, they would rather inherit relatively intact cities, industries, roads and railways than a nuclear wasteland. Soviet planning therefore seems more directed to a controlled invasion by conventional forces which would overwhelm NATO by sheer weight of numbers and sacrificial speed of movement – airborne forces from the sky and naval brigades from the sea to seize key objectives coinciding with a massive armoured *Blitzkrieg*. Chemical and biological agents would also be extensively used. Tactical nuclear weapons would, inevitably, come into play because the vastly outnumbered NATO forces in Europe could not hope to contain such an assault for more than a few hours – days at best – without resorting to short range missiles such as Lance.

A build-up to a Soviet invasion would be characterized initially by a wave of civil disruption – strikes, go-slows, lock-outs and lock-ins, protest marches and the like. In this sense democracy is in some ways its own worst enemy. Perfectly genuine trades union and civil rights leaders could be manoeuvred into situations orchestrated from Moscow and their followers would probably go blindly along as always. Communications, oil, chemical, electronics and power industries would be worst hit, for obvious reasons, followed by the emergency services. Whether Spetsnaz personnel would be actively involved in this phase of operations is unanswerable, but they certainly would be in the second phase. This would take the form of a wave of terrorist attacks by home-grown organizations many of which are funded and equipped – even if half the time they do not know it – from Moscow. The pattern would not be identical within each country or it would be too obvious and could provoke the threat at least of a pre-emptive strike by NATO.

It is into such a destabilized situation that Spetsnaz 'diversionary' teams not already in place would be infiltrated, clandestinely at first and then more overtly as the countdown towards full-scale military action entered its last hours. Many would wear NATO uniforms to add to the confusion. Their overall effect on the purely military side of the situation would probably not be that enormous, but on top of a wave of industrial unrest and apparently indiscriminate bombing by terrorist groups, their attacks on both hard (military) and soft (political and scientific) targets would be aimed at further undermining the morale of the general population, sapping the will to fight which is so crucial to victory. Speed and surprise are the watchwords of Soviet military planning, as in the event of an invasion of western Europe their main concern would be to present the United States with a *fait accompli* within less than a week so as to minimize the risk of nuclear escalation.

What most of the members of these 'diversionary' groups probably do not realize is that the Soviet High Command regards them as expendable. In Norway or Turkey, which are relatively under-populated and have vast stretches of rugged, uninhabited terrain, the teams would stand a good chance of being able to 'disappear' once their objectives had been accomplished. Faced with the density of a hostile population in Germany or Britain, for example, and with trained counter-terrorist squads dogging their heels, they would have little chance of survival once they had exposed their presence. Nevertheless, as history has proved so many times, men *are* prepared to sacrifice themselves for what they consider the right cause, and Spetsnaz troops are the most highly motivated and self-disciplined in the Soviet armed forces.

The Spetsnaz long-range reconnaissance units, on the other hand, would stand an excellent chance of both carrying out their missions and surviving. They appear to be trained more for war in the east than the west, and in the event of a war with China would certainly operate deep within the vast and wild hinterland of the People's Republic just as they did during the Soviet invasion of Manchuria in 1945. Then, only about twenty teams, thirty to forty men strong, were deployed, some dropping by parachute close to important cities such as Harbin, Mukden, Chanchun and Port Arthur and others being landed by sea. Their effect on the overall military situation was relatively slight, but the appearance of Russian troops so far in their rear areas caused a great deal of panic in the Japanese army of occupation. The deployment of greater numbers of Spetsnaz teams in any future conflict, with modern arms and training, would undoubtedly have a much greater effect, especially if followed up by full-scale attacks by regular airborne and naval infantry forces.

Japan is another obvious target for Spetsnaz forces in the Far East, for it would be vital in time of war with the United States for the Soviet Union to take out airfields and ports as quickly as possible so as to give them control of the Tsugaru, Soya and Tsushima Straits. Without this, the Soviet Pacific Fleet which is based in Vladivostock could only operate with extreme difficulty. American naval installations such as that at Yokosuka would be priorities, and it is probable that Subic Bay in the Philippines, Guam and even Pearl Harbor are also Spetsnaz targets[17].

It is impossible to quantify the effect Spetsnaz teams could have during a full-scale war as opposed to a more localized conflict in, say, Africa, the Middle East or South America (where they predominantly operate as advisors and instructors in any case). Certainly the Soviet Union values them, if only as a relatively inexpensive weapon whose *potential* to damage the enemy is high in relation to their numbers. Much is often made of the fact that the Russian soldier is a conscript, and therefore less well disciplined and motivated than his counterpart in a volunteer army. What is conveniently forgotten is that any conscript army contains a proportion of men who would have been volunteers in any case, and this is certain to apply to those who persevere through the gruelling Spetsnaz training programme. It is also said that Spetsnaz troops cannot be as skilled as their western counterparts, because they cannot possibly be as well trained within the short two-year conscription period, even allowing for the fact that they are allowed no leave. Those who profess this view neglect the fact that the majority of officers and NCOs in Spetsnaz, as well as a high proportion of the Private soldiers, are men who have chosen the army (or navy) as a career, so will normally have considerably more than two years' experience before they are allowed to go on an overseas mission.

What is certain is that western military strategists and planners have, over recent years, come to see Spetsnaz as a very real threat. As a result, home defence forces, both military and police, are increasingly being trained to seek out and destroy them. During exercises, members of the SAS and other western special forces take on the role of Spetsnaz teams and attack command and communications posts in the field – with, it is said but not officially admitted, a considerable measure of success. The effects of Spetsnaz attacks on behind-the-lines targets, both military and civilian, are calculated into wargames. In 1985, for example, SAS and SBS teams both took part in Exercise 'Brave

Defender', a massive wargame designed to test Britain's defences against an all-out attack by conventional forces. Both the Territorial Army and the police were involved as well as the Royal Observer Corps, but it was reported that the special forces' teams scored something like ninety per cent in penetrating to their targets. Security has been tightened up subsequently, but one is forced to wonder whether this would be sufficient.

* * *

Spetsnaz is not the only elite behind the lines force available to the Soviet Union in time of war. In 1973 the East German Nationale Volksarmee (NVA – National People's Army) created the 40th Fallschirmjäger (Parachute) Battalion which has the honorary title 'Willi Sanger' and is organized and trained along Spetsnaz lines. The battalion is specifically dedicated to targets in West Germany and its personnel have an obvious advantage over Soviet Spetsnaz teams in that they speak the same language. Personnel are recruited at the age of eighteen and serve for a minimum of three years, but as in Russia the NVA takes care to nurture career soldiers. A former member of the British Special Boat Squadron, whose name must for obvious reasons remain anonymous, rates the 'Willi Sanger' Battalion 'the best operational airborne unit in training and active service within the SovBloc countries'.

According to East German defector Rainer Paul Fuller, the battalion trains at the Edgar-Andrae Ausbildungszentrale (Edgar-Andrae Training Centre) deep in a forest near the garrison town of Lehnin, close to the Berlin-Dessau railway line[18]. This is officially run by the Gesellschaft für Sport und Technik (Association for Sport and Technology), nominally a youth organization like the Russian DOSAAF but actually a recruiting front. The NVA shares the camp with the Hauptverwaltung Aufklärung (HVA – Chief Administration, Intelligence), East Germany's equivalent of Britain's DI6 or the American CIA, responsible for training and infiltrating agents and sleepers. The battalion's garrison is at Prora on the island of Rugen in the Baltic.

It is rare for precise documentation of Warsaw Pact special forces to fall into Western hands, but we were fortunate enough to secure a copy of the NVA Paratroopers' Handbook, from which the following extracts revealing the functions of the 'Willi Sanger' Battalion have been translated. They demonstrate a singular ruthlessness of purpose and methods as well as the existence within West Germany of a well-established sleeper network of guerrillas who would spring into action when 'woken' by Moscow.

The translation is literal, rather than 'tidied up', since we felt this gives it greater immediacy.

'LL [*Luftlande* – air landing] paratroopers should, during a time of war and also during periods of suspense and tension, spread terror and implement acts of sabotage in the enemy's territory [the Federal Republic of Germany, Belgium and Holland]. Tasks to be carried out are the destruction of the atomic deployment means, the prevention or delay of the enemy marching up, the destruction of enemy command posts, the interruption or destruction of enemy communications centres, the interruption or prevention of provisions to enemy forces, the switching off of important air defence systems [and] the assassination or abduction of important commanding figures.

'If a paratroop group suddenly meets with a relatively weak enemy and cannot get out of the way in time, then, without any consideration, he is to be exterminated. In such a case, no enemy soldier may escape.

'An enemy who has recognized the group must under all circumstances be eliminated. Firearms may only be used if there are no other alternatives. If in a certain situation it is not possible to get by a guard unnoticed, then he is to be exterminated so silently that [the act] will be discovered as late as possible.

'The paratroops will, above all, be deployed to fight objectives within enemy territorial lines. They have predominantly to fight such objects as will influence the course and outcome of an encounter.

'Enemy forces should be destroyed at close range by short bursts of fire, by hand grenades or in close hand-to-hand combat. The paratroops should only attack when the situation deems it necessary.

'Speed and violence are life-savers!'

Later, the same document details procedures for infiltrating the troops into NATO convoys, particularly of nuclear missile carriers, using stolen vehicles.

'If guards are to be reckoned with, wait for a break in the convoy in the corresponding direction of traffic and filter in or follow on. At signs of the convoy coming to a halt, leave immediately. In the vicinity of the action, the vehicles must be well hidden. Under no circumstances may the troops start up the hidden vehicles.'

As for the existence of a Communist fifth column, the handbook states: 'Before the deployment of the LL para-troops, the commander can obtain addresses of responsible persons who can support them. Care must be taken, the area observed and secured and the password asked for carefully. Encounters can be organized for the paratroops to meet with guerrilla units.'

This paragraph clearly indicates that an organized pro-Soviet underground guerrilla movement already exists in West Germany which can be called upon to co-operate in time of crisis, confrontation or war. Some of these people will simply be 'fellow travellers', useless in a military situation other than for their local knowledge. Others will be in charge of concealed caches of weapons and explosives, while the key minority will be sleepers infiltrated into place months or years beforehand and will have had the same sort of training as the Spetsnaz and LL troops themselves.

Training for the sleeper role is also carried out at the 'Franz Mehring' Institute in East Berlin, courses lasting a minimum of twelve months. Close by, in Schmerwitz, is the 'Ernst Thalmann' School for working men's commandos, popularly known as the 'Techno Kommandos'. Graduates are found jobs in West Germany under cover identities, but their real task in time of war would be the destruction of observation posts, radio and radar stations and air defence installations. Another piece of generally classified information which found its way into our hands is headed 'VVS Nr G 572910' and entitled 'The acts carried out by units of the Border Guards in combat defence for the establishment of defence back-ups at the Company base and for taking objectives occupied by the enemy'.

Although we are unable to quote from this for security reasons because it identifies some Western defence pro-cedures, it outlines the equipment and *modus operandi* of the Grenzaufklärer, or Border Reconnaissance units. Just as in Russia the border guards are controlled by the KGB, so in East Germany they are run by the Ministerium für Staats-Sicherheit (MfS – Ministry for State Security). Their normal task is to supplement the work of the regular border guards in photographing anyone on the western side of the wire who appears to be taking an undue interest in East German border installations. In time of war one of their tasks would be to infiltrate the border areas of West Germany in advance of the main striking forces. They also have a defensive role in helping to protect sensitive radio and radar installations close to the border and destroying them if necessary to prevent them falling into NATO hands. Obviously, Grenzaufklärer personnel are thoroughly vetted for political allegiance, since with their training, defection would be comparatively simple.

Although East German special forces are therefore small in numbers compared to their Soviet counterparts, they are an active and vital component in the overall Warsaw Pact line-up.

The armies of the other Warsaw Pact nations are considered less politically reliable than that of East Germany. Over the years, popular uprisings have been brutally suppressed in Czechoslovakia, Hungary and Poland, uprisings in which some members of the national armed forces took part. Nevertheless, Poland has its equivalent of Spetsnaz in the 401st Parachute Battalion, nominally part of the 6th Pomeranian Air Assault Division. Little is known of this formation except that it falls under the command of the *Wojskowa Sluzba Wewnetrzna* (WSW – Army Security Service, equivalent of the GRU) and that some of its personnel were involved in the arrest and trial of four security police officers who murdered pro-Solidarity priest Father Jerzy Popieluszko in 1985. In Czechoslovakia the 22nd Airborne Brigade (which is actually only the size of a reinforced regiment, perhaps 1,000-strong) is said to contain a 'special operations' battalion, but no details are available. Hungary has a single airborne battalion some 400 men strong but it is unknown whether this, or part of it, is tasked for Spetsnaz-type long-range penetration missions. The same applies to the Romanian and Bulgarian Armies which both include a single parachute regiment.

Notes Chapter Two

[1] Adapted from a literal translation by the Soviet Studies Centre, Royal Military Academy Sandhurst.

2 *Operations in the enemy rear: Soviet doctrine and tactics*, Soviet Studies Centre, Royal Military Academy Sandhurst, page 16.

3 Kharchenko was killed in 1975, by then with the rank of Marshal, while testing an unspecified new weapon.

4 Although aerials are quickly and easily replaceable, a radar post in particular only needs to be knocked out for a couple of minutes under the right circumstances for an enemy to get through to his target.

5 Volume 7, 1979.

6 From *Soviet Military Power*.

7 6 September 1984.

8 Probably Mil Mi-8s, designated 'Hip' by NATO. These helicopters are powered by twin 1,500 shp engines which give a top speed of 230 km/h, hovering ceiling of 4,500 m and range of 360 km. They have a crew of two and can carry up to 32 fully-armed troops, although 28 is a more usual number. Additionally, they can be fitted with guided anti-tank missiles or unguided anti-personnel rockets on fuselage pylons.

9 Confirmed by Red Cross reports.

10 Volume XI, Issue 6, 1987.

11 This remark suggests that the magazine was confusing ordinary air mobile forces with Spetsnaz, who in common with Western special forces normally operate in linked teams of four men operating independently or interdependently. In Afghanistan, Spetsnaz troops functioned closely alongside the ordinary airborne forces, so confusion is easily understandable.

12 There is no exact equivalent to the Soviet 'front', but in simple terms it is a group of four to five armies, one of which will be armoured. A Soviet 'theatre' consists of three or more fronts plus a fleet. Thus, for example, the twenty-plus divisions which form the 'Group of Soviet Forces Germany' would be designated a 'front' in time of war and together with the northern (Polish) and central (Czechoslovakian) groups would become a 'theatre'.

13 The Dienst Sicherheitspolitik, a West German studies centre based in Bonn comparable to the Institute of Strategic Studies but specializing in security matters.

14 'Voluntary Society for Co-operation with the Army, Air Force and

Fleet'; not quite a cadet corps in the Western sense, more of a 'militarized' Boy Scout organization. See also Chapter Seven.

[15] The parachute used in training is the PD-47 which has a diameter of ten metres and gives a rate of descent of just over five metres a second, minimum jump height being 300 m. After basic training Spetsnaz personnel graduate to the more modern RS-1 which is easier to steer and has a slightly slower rate of descent. For special missions where pin-point accuracy is required, Spetsnaz personnel may use the UT-15, a high performance parachute developed from sporting designs which requires a great deal of skill to control.

[16] Nuclear, Biological and Chemical. In line with the troops of most modern armies, Spetsnaz frequently train wearing full NBC protection suits (popularly known as 'Noddy suits'), often wearing them for prolonged periods. Apart possibly from China, Russia is the country which takes biological and chemical warfare most seriously and practices its use as well as deploying large numbers of decontamination units in exercises. NATO countries – so far as is admitted – only practice *defensive* techniques against such weapons.

[17] US Naval Institute *Proceedings*, August 1987.

[18] In Brandenburg, principal recruiting area in Nazi Germany for the famous wartime Brandenburg Regiment which pioneered so many of the behind the lines penetration and deception techniques subsequently adopted by the special forces of other nations.

Chapter Three

The spider in the web

Two organizations rest at the centre of what has often been aptly called the Soviet 'spider's web' of global infiltration, subversion and espionage. First is the KGB, the *Komitet Gosudarstvennoi Bezopastnosti* or Committee for State Security, and second the GRU, the *Glavnoye Razvedyvatel-noye Upravlenie*, the Chief Intelligence Directorate of the Soviet General Staff, one of whose many functions is recruiting, training and running Spetsnaz. Since all their energies are devoted ultimately to the same ends, no single element can be viewed in isolation. However, since extensive books and articles on the histories, organization and function of both the KGB and the GRU have already been written, only a résumé will be given here.

The KGB

The KGB is the largest, most widely feared and amongst the most cruel of intelligence and counter-intelligence agencies the world has ever seen and, whether he realizes it or not, the KGB controls every aspect of a Soviet citizen's life from the moment he is born until the day he dies. The KGB is a private army, a secret police force, a border guard, an administrator of 'psychiatric hospitals', and the instrument through which the Soviet government foments economic and political instability worldwide.

The KGB was created in the wake of the Russian Revolution by a former Polish nobleman, Felix Dzerzhinsky, as 'an organ for the revolutionary settlement of accounts with counter-revolutionaries'. Over the succeeding years it has had many changes of name – Cheka, GPU, OGPU, NKVD and NKGB, MVD and MGB – but it has been the KGB since 1954 and will be referred to as such throughout. Its directors have, between them, been ultimately responsible for the deaths of more people than the leaders of Nazi Germany ever dreamed of.

Dzerzhinsky was succeeded by Vyacheslav Menzhinsky whose greatest coup was setting up the apparatus which recruited the so-called 'Cambridge Spy Ring' – Burgess, Maclean, Philby, Blunt and, so it is claimed by Chapman Pincher and Peter Wright, Sir Roger Hollis, a former head of MI5. Menzhinsky was briefly followed by Genrikh Yagoda and then by Nikolai Yezhov, the 'bloody dwarf' who orchestrated the Tukachevsky Purge in 1937 which decimated the leadership of the Red Army. Yezhov's own successor, Lavrenti Beria, was Stalin's spymaster throughout the Second World War and attempted to seize the reins of power himself on his master's death but was murdered by a cabal of Soviet officers.

Beria was followed by Ivan Serov, the man who had been responsible for the Katyn Forest massacre in 1940[1], then by Alexandr Shelepin and next by the man who would later achieve Beria's dream of supreme power, Yuri Andropov. Andropov first leapt into prominence in 1956 when, as a Soviet Counsellor in Budapest, he was largely responsible for the brutal suppression of the Hungarian uprising. As director of the KGB he was ruthless in his efforts at suppressing dissidents through the use of drugs in psychiatric hospitals. The Soviet leadership tried to 'whitewash' his image before electing him General Secretary of the Communist Party but the majority of the Western media was not taken in and, although precise details of his career are hazy, he was every bit as dedicated to the ideal of a world ruled along Soviet lines as any of his predecessors. Leadership of the KGB then briefly passed to General Vitaly Fedorchuk but this was only an interim appointment and from the end of 1982 to 1 October 1988 the KGB was ruled by Viktor Chebrikov. On that date Mr Gorbachev replaced him with 64-year-old Vladimir Kryuchkav.

The KGB employs some 400,000 men and women, excluding informers (even Russians joke that whenever three Muscovites meet, at least one works for the KGB). Of these, however, only some 25,000 are believed to be directly involved in foreign intelligence work.

Top of the ladder in the KGB hierarchy is the First Chief Directorate, housed no longer in Dzerzhinsky Square in the centre of Moscow, above the notorious Lubyanka Prison, but in a modern office block off the Moscow ring road near the village of Tëplyystan. It is screened by woods and approached by a narrow access road guarded at all times by armed soldiers wearing militia uniforms but whose bearing and alertness reveals they are far from mere militia. A sign over the entrance in the formidable barbed wire fence surrounding the complex declares it to be the 'Scientific Research Centre'. Above ground it is a seven-storey building in the shape of a three-pointed star but this is only the tip of an iceberg for its most sensitive offices are buried deep in the earth and hardened against nuclear attack.

The First Chief Directorate is responsible for foreign intelligence and is itself divided into three sub-Directorates, three Services and a fluctuating number of other Departments. Directorate S is the largest of these and is responsible for running the KGB's network of 'illegals'[2] around the world. A great deal of its work lies in preparing detailed cover stories and documents for people who will have to live and work in the West for many years. It also runs a network of training schools and camps in Russia and the Soviet Bloc countries. Directorate T, second of the sub-Directorates, shares the responsibility for scientific and industrial espionage with the GRU. Apart from assigning experts to Soviet embassies, it is also responsible for analysing and collating the vast amount of information freely published around the world in technical books and magazines; this duty is shared with the State Committee on Science and Technology and with the Academy of Sciences. Most KGB 'legals' are members of Directorate T. The third sub-Directorate, K, is responsible for penetrating foreign intelligence agencies and has had some of the KGB's most notable successes, as witnessed by the number of spy scandals and trials in America, Britain, France, West Germany and elsewhere since the 1940s. Directorate K is also largely responsible for infiltrating and encouraging terrorist organizations harmful to the West, for keeping surveillance on Soviet citizens abroad and for internal security within the KGB itself.

The First Chief Directorate's Service I is charged with analysing the vast flow of information coming into headquarters from innumerable sources, legitimate and clandestine, and for preparing twice-monthly intelligence digests for the Politburo. Service A is the KGB's disinformation department, responsible for propaganda and generally helping promote agitation and unrest, using Western peace movements, trades unions and other left-wing organizations as its tools. The Soviet press agencies, Tass and Novosti, are both controlled by Service A[3]. Service R is the operational planning section of the First Chief Directorate and was brought into being in the 1970s to prevent wastage through duplication of effort by agents in the field.

Apart from these six sub-Directorates and Services, the First Chief Directorate also contains a number of Departments, eleven being allocated specific geographical areas to infiltrate at every level of life. Each Department is further sub-divided into Desks responsible either for individual countries or for key cities within those countries, such as London, Washington, Bonn or Tokyo, for example. These Departments are as follows:

Department number	*Area of responsibility*
1	North America
2	Central and South America
3	Australia, New Zealand, Scandinavia and the UK
4	Austria and West Germany
5	Belgium, France, Holland, Ireland, Italy, Luxembourg and Spain
6	China, Kampuchea, North Korea and Vietnam
7	Indonesia, Japan, the Philippines, Singapore and Thailand
8	Afghanistan, Albania, Greece, the Middle East including Iran and Turkey, and Yugoslavia
9	English-speaking African nations
10	French-speaking African nations
17	Bangladesh, India, Pakistan and Sri Lanka[4]

Department 11 is the liaison unit with the intelligence agencies of other Warsaw Pact countries – and also spies on them and ensures they follow the Moscow line on important issues. Department 12 is an elite formation created by Andropov to make use of older agents with wide experience who would normally have been retired. Given new status and diplomatic immunity as part of trade and scientific missions, they have a watching brief and are trusted sufficiently to be allowed close contacts in the West. There is no Department 13, although it is doubtful whether superstition plays any part in this! It used to exist, but then became Department V, the 'dirty tricks' department responsible for *Mokrei dela* ('wet jobs', KGB slang for assassinations, the equivalent of the CIA's 'terminating with extreme prejudice'). After the defection of Oleg Lyalin was revealed in 1971, Department V suffered a very thorough internal housekeeping and became Department 8 of Directorate S – not to be confused with the geographical Department 8 tabulated above.

Department 14 is 'special effects' and supplies the miniature cameras, microphones and other tools of spycraft, including lasers which can be used to eavesdrop on a conversation in a room by picking up the minute vibrations in window panes; weapons; drugs and poisons; radios; microdot processors, etc. Department 15 is clerical while Department 16 is codes and ciphers. However, it in turn should not be confused with the Eighth Chief Directorate (see below), for its sole task is to recruit code and cipher personnel from foreign intelligence agencies. Finally there is the unnumbered Personnel Department, of which Chebrikov was the former head, which is responsible for recruitment into the KGB.

With the exception of the Eighth Chief Directorate, tasked with creating KGB codes and ciphers, with signals security and with monitoring Western transmissions (a function it shares with the GRU's 6th Directorate), the other KGB formations are primarily concerned with internal security. The Second Chief Directorate runs the huge network of informers and local KGB offices throughout the USSR, and monitors the activities of Western visitors. The Third Directorate spies on the GRU and the armed forces. There is no Fourth or Sixth Directorate. The Fifth, created by Andropov, monitors and controls Soviet dissidents; the Seventh undertakes surveillance of foreign embassies and diplomats in Moscow, while the Ninth is responsible for providing bodyguards and other security measures for high ranking Soviet officials both at home and abroad. Finally there is the unnumbered Border Guards Directorate described in the previous chapter. Guardianship of the gulags is entrusted to the MVD, which retained its semi-autonomous status after Stalin's death.

Over the years the KGB has recruited agents and implanted illegals around the world and those who defect or are caught must necessarily only be a fraction of the total numbers involved. The principal evidence about their operations and methods comes either from that published during court cases, from the memoirs of defectors and people previously involved in Western intelligence agencies (who often have personal axes to grind and whose testimony must therefore often be taken with a proverbial pinch of salt), and from dissidents who succeed in smuggling evidence to the West via conduits such as Amnesty International.

Apart from the infamous Cambridge Spy Ring whose history is well known, especially since the so-called Philby 'revelations' in *The Sunday Times* in spring 1988, celebrated espionage cases involving the KGB include (in America) those of Judy Coplon, Alger Hiss, 'Rudolph Herrmann' (real name Ludek Zemenek and chief KGB illegal first in Canada and then in America), his wife Inga and son Peter, and Sergeant Robert Lee Johnson; in France, Georges Pacques; in Canada, Professor Hugh Hambleton, a man specifically entrusted with student recruitment in universities; and in West Germany, Günther Guillaume, Willy Brandt's confidante. People blackmailed into spying, or whom the KGB tried to blackmail, have included RAF technician Douglas Britten in 1968, Maurice Dejean, French Ambassador to Moscow, in 1963, and the British Ambassador, Sir Geoffrey Harrison, in 1968; German Foreign Ministry secretary Leonore Heinz[5] (and a succession of other girls lured by infatuation) in 1967 and Admiral Hermann Lüdke who committed suicide in 1969.

The KGB has also had its defectors, several of them foreign nationals because the Soviet Union often uses such people from other Warsaw Pact countries because they are thought to be less suspect than native Russians: Petr Deriabin in 1954, Joseph Frolik in 1968 (the man who implicated British Labour MPs Tom Driberg, Will Owen and John Stonehouse and exposed RAF technician Nicholas Prager); Jan Sejna and Major Ladislav Bittman in the same year; Oleg Lyalin in 1971, Viktor Lessiovski in 1973 and Stanislav Levchenko in 1979. Two of the most significant defections apart from that of Lyalin were those of Bogdan Stashinky, a KGB assassin who made a full confession in open court in Karlsruhe after his West German girlfriend persuaded him to give himself up, and Nicolai Chochlov, another assassin who handed over to the West German police the gun and cyanide-tipped bullets with which he had been ordered to kill Russian emigré Georgi

Okolovitch. These revelations on top of Lyalin's, added to the murder by ricin[6] poisoning of BBC commentator Georgi Markov in 1978 by the Bulgarian secret service, show clearly that murder *is* a tool used by the SovBloc agencies to silence those opposed to them. The particular relevance of this factual, confessed and documented evidence is shown in Chapter Eight.

All of the above are just examples of cases with which most readers will be familiar, or will at least have heard of, but they cover a spread of over thirty years and demonstrate that Soviet infiltration of the West is neither new nor something that stopped with the death of Stalin. Whenever there is any fairly long time gap in the security services' apprehension of agents or traitors, the average person tends to think that the house has been cleaned and that there is nothing more to worry about. Unfortunately, this is far from being the case, regardless of the public image projected by Mr Gorbachev. (Remember, Nikita Kruschev adopted the same approach while simultaneously shipping nuclear missiles into Cuba and bringing the world closer to a nuclear confrontation than was – or is – attractive to contemplate.)

In March and April 1988, the two biggest spy scandals to rock Europe for years burst into the headlines in Britain and West Germany. Both involved hi-tech projects at the same sort of level which has enabled the Soviet Union to build a fighter aircraft like the MiG-29 'Fulcrum' which drew such crowds at Farnborough later in the same year – even though the expert concensus is that the aircraft is still not up to the standard of current Western fighters.

On 20 March it was first publicly revealed that a 43-year-old secretary, Elke Falk, who worked for the Ministry for Economic Co-operation in Bonn, had been arrested and charged with espionage. Like so many other women over the years, particularly in West Germany, she had been seduced by a smooth-talking KGB agent going under the name Gerhard Thieme and became so infatuated that for several years she had been passing him copies of documents from her office, which sometimes included cabinet briefing papers. Her arrest led to several others over the next few days, and Hans Gert Lange, official spokesman for the *Bundesamt für Verfassungsschutz* (BfV – literally 'Office for the Protection of the Constitution' but actually West Germany's equivalent of DI5), said he expected 'many more' similar cases in the future.

Writing in *The Sunday Times* on 27 March, Simon Freeman said that women like Falk 'are victims of a huge KGB-Warsaw Pact intelligence gathering effort, particularly in West Germany, which is based on the "vacuum cleaner" approach, the assumption that all information, most of it not remotely secret, is vital because knowledge is power.'

Quoting a 'security source', Mr Freeman wrote:

'The Russians want to know everything about the West. Often it is scientific and technological information. Sometimes it is not even secret. But the Russians do not care. Most of all they want to get inside our government to find out what is being said and what is being argued.

'No-one', Mr Freeman concluded, 'least of all West German counter-intelligence, believes the KGB will ever be defeated. "We are a democracy and we are the front line with the East," said one source. "They will go on and on. All we can do is to work harder." '

The men arrested following Elke Falk included Austrian-born Helmut Kolasch, a 44-year-old businessman who is alleged to have been a Soviet agent since 1971 and to have passed on secrets relating to both the Panavia Tornado and the new European Fighter Project. The BfV uncovered a coding pad concealed in a record sleeve in his flat. The others were Fajardo Amaya, a Colombian-born engineer who studied in East Germany and is said to have been an active KGB agent since 1981; Peter Friesen, a Soviet-born engineer who has passed on information on West German political parties; Georg Bender, another Soviet-born engineer said to have been recruited in 1974, sent into West Germany three years later after training and to have given the KGB sensitive information on electronic projects in the Karlsruhe firm he worked for; Edmund Neufert, a Soviet-born teacher of Russian at a language school for civil servants just outside Cologne; and Simon Or, another teacher who moved to West Germany from Israel in the late 1970s. He is alleged to have had meetings with KGB agents but is not believed to have passed on any classified documents.

These arrests are a considerable embarrassment to Bonn following the 'house cleaning' within the BfV resulting from the defection of the head of its East German Desk, Hans-Joachim Tiedge, in 1985, and the arrest of Messerschmitt-Bölkow-

Blohm's research director, Manfred Rotsch, in 1986. (He was sentenced to eight years' imprisonment but exchanged in a spy swap after only a year.) Dr Gerhard Boeden, head of the BfV, said that the current 'thaw' between Moscow and Washington has resulted in 'much more active' spying activities by the Warsaw Pact.

The German arrests in March were followed within days by the arrest in England on 3 April of a 42-year-old Czech national posing as a Dutch art dealer under the name Erwin van Haarlem. He had been in England for three years and was put under surveillance by DI5 for some six months before being arrested. British intelligence agents staked out a flat overlooking van Haarlem's in Friern Barnet, North London, using electronic surveillance equipment and video cameras. When they searched his flat after his arrest by Special Branch (for DI5 has no powers of arrest), the intelligence men are said to have uncovered coding and deciphering equipment, and van Haarlem was subsequently charged at Bow Street court under Section 7 of the 1920 Official Secrets Act. The specific charges were of recording coded information and possessing equipment to decipher it.

To begin with the Czech Embassy denied knowing anything about van Haarlem but after he was charged they complained to the Foreign Office about the way he had been treated!

There was considerable press speculation at the time that van Haarlem might have been another Gordon Lonsdale – the man at the centre of the Portland Spy Ring in the 1950s – and attention focused on the Admiralty underwater research unit in Bath, but to date no further arrests have been notified. The van Haarlem case also renewed discussion of the possibility of another 'mole' in the Government Communications Headquarters (GCHQ) at Cheltenham, something which has been feared ever since the Geoffrey Prime trial in 1982, but again nothing has so far emerged[7]. If there *are* agents or illegals in place, they have probably been ordered to keep a low profile for a while.

Curiously, according to *The Daily Telegraph* Information Bureau, since April 1988 the van Haarlem story has 'sunk without trace'. This suggests either that he has been 'turned' and after debriefing will emerge with a new identity, or that he has been quietly exchanged for one of our own agents.

* * *

The Portland case which broke in 1961 involved a former naval Petty Officer, Harry Houghton, who had secured a job with the secret Underwater Weapons Establishment at Portland, Dorset, in 1952 and commenced spying for the Soviet Union some four years later. The levers were money and a Polish mistress who knew of some of his earlier black market dealings in Warsaw. His controller went under the name Gordon Lonsdale but he was actually a GRU officer, Konon Molodi. Born in Russia and educated in California, he had fought with the Red Army during the war but was sent back to the West in 1954 using the identity of a Canadian who had actually been killed fighting in Finland. Others involved were a Jewish couple, Morris and Lena Cohen, who had earlier narrowly escaped being implicated in the 'atom spy' trials in the United States and possibly being executed alongside their friends Julius and Ethel Rosenberg. This couple, better known to the world as Peter and Helen Kroger, were the link between Houghton and Lonsdale. All received jail sentences of 15 to 25 years, but Lonsdale was exchanged for Greville Wynne in 1964, the Krogers for Gerald Brooke in 1969 and Houghton and his girlfriend 'Bunty' Gee were released to write their colourful memoirs after only ten years.

All the details of Britain's latest submarine and anti-submarine equipment and techniques, added to the success (before they were ultimately detected) of the 'atom spies' who gave Russia the ability to catch up with America and Britain years before anyone expected them to, heaped kudos on the head of the KGB's Cinderella sister service, the GRU. Far less well known generally in the West than 'big brother', the GRU is smaller but no less efficient. In many ways it may be *more* efficient. It has, so far as we are aware, only had one high-ranking mole within its ranks, Colonel Oleg Penkovsky, who was executed after a show trial; and one major defector, a man who goes under the pseudonym Viktor Suvorov and who has written several purportedly factual books about the Red Army, the GRU and Spetsnaz (see bibliography).

The trouble with Suvorov's books is that, in our experience, they are a minefield of misinformation for the unwary, although useful if you are selective. Suvorov is totally biased against the Soviet regime and this comes through in his vindictive style. He is not always accurate. For example – and it was this which first started us really doubting him – he writes at length about Spetsnaz involvement in sporting

activities within and outside the USSR. If you believe
Suvorov, a high proportion of Soviet athletes who are allowed
to compete at international level are actually members of
Spetsnaz and use their sporting accomplishments to make
contact with people in the West and familiarize themselves
with the 'outside' environment. To a degree Suvorov's
assertions are undoubtedly true. Members of the armed forces
of most countries compete in amateur athletics at various
levels, and many are of international or Olympic standard.
Some Russian athletes, by a simple process of elimination,
must therefore be members of Spetsnaz. But a majority?

Where Suvorov fell down badly on page 104 of *Inside the
Soviet Army* was in claiming that a Spetsnaz Lieutenant,
Valentin Yerikalin, won a silver medal for rowing in the 1968
Olympics. This supposed fact has been widely quoted
subsequently.

No-one called Valentin Yerikalin, even allowing for
romanization of the Cyrillic alphabet, has *ever* won *any* medal
in *any* Olympic games …

The obvious question is, did Suvorov make a simple and
understandable mistake – or not? Did he fall down, or was he
pushed? If you think about it, any book which a defector
writes for general publication is going to be heavily vetted by
the security services of the country in which he has sought
asylum – in Suvorov's case, the UK. They will have a vested
interest in two ways. Firstly, the defector must not be allowed
to pass coded information back to his former employers. This
is a natural precaution because any defector is always
regarded with intense suspicion in case he is a 'double'.
Secondly, a defector's memoirs can be used by the security
services to pass on disinformation. Obviously, Suvorov could
not tell the GRU anything it did not already know about its
own organization, structure or methods. What he *could* do
was give the GRU the impression that he had revealed less
during his debriefing than they might have expected, even to
the extent of falsifying information. This would then,
hopefully, lead the GRU to believe that NATO knew less
about them than they feared. The really tortuous mind might
finally ask, why leave such an obvious piece of false
information lying where it could so easily be checked – even if
no-one, to our knowledge, has so far done so? Was the name
'Valentin Yerikalin' the key to a code which only the GRU
could read, despite all Western precautions?

The GRU

The GRU is the single largest and most powerful military intelligence agency in the world. A child of the Bolshevik Revolution, it was officially called into being by Lenin on 21 October 1918 under pressure from the head of the Red Army, Leon Trotsky. It was initially given the innocuous title 'Registered Directorate of the Workers' and Peasants' Red Army'; this was later changed to 'Registrational Directorate of the Field Staff of the Republic' and finally to 'Chief Intelligence Directorate of the General Staff'.

From the very beginning there was intense rivalry – indeed, hatred – between Soviet Army intelligence and the Cheka (which eventually became the KGB). This led to a purge of Red Army intelligence officers in 1920 in which hundreds were executed but the GRU as a whole survived. By the early 1930s it was the most powerful intelligence agency in the world, with an overseas budget substantially larger than that of the OGPU (KGB) and a worldwide network of illegals. The reason for the size and determination of the GRU's overseas effort was simple. At the time of the Revolution Russia was a primitive country by European or American standards and although valiant steps were being taken to haul industry up by its bootstraps, the only way the Russians could secure the modern technology they needed was by buying or stealing it. Even though their own technology is now of a high order and there is nothing second rate about their scientists the Soviets still operate on the principle that it is often cheaper to steal technology than to spend huge sums on their own research.

Ever paranoid, Stalin first used the GRU to 'clean up' the NKVD in 1935-36 then turned the latter organization loose on the Red Army in 1937, two purges which denuded the Soviet Union of some of its most talented officers and helped account for Russian reverses when Germany attacked in 1941.

The GRU as we know it today emerged from the power struggle which followed Stalin's death in 1953 as an independent but subordinate agency to the KGB, and indeed the head of the GRU is always a KGB appointment. It is responsible for *all* forms of military intelligence inside and outside the USSR, Army, Navy, Air Force, electronic and space (the last being called 'cosmic intelligence' by the Russians), and also controls a vast network of military attachés and undercover agents around the world. Its chief

Director – currently General Petr Ivanovich Ivashutin – is responsible for broad policy decisions and personally directs a network of the most capable agents and illegals. His deputy controls four of the six main Directorates, each of which is in turn run by a Colonel-General.

The 1st Directorate is responsible for Europe, excluding the UK; the 2nd for the UK, North and South America, Australia and New Zealand; the 3rd for Asia and the 4th for Africa. In addition there are four departments called Directions operating independently of the Directorates, and which often overlap their functions, which also report directly to the Deputy Director. Each Direction is headed by a Lieutenant-General. The 1st is Moscow and controls all GRU agents operating in the capital, in science and industry for example. The 2nd is Berlin and controls a large network of undercover agents in all four sectors of this particularly sensitive city. The 3rd Direction is responsible for supporting the various terrorist 'liberation' movements around the world, for supplying them with instructors (many of whom are Spetsnaz), money and arms. The 4th operates out of Cuba into Central America and the Caribbean in liaison with the Cuban secret service, the *Dirección General de Inteligencia* (DGI).

The Deputy Director is also in charge of the training centres for undercover agents, both Russian and foreign. In these centres which have been described by defectors, including Suvorov, agents live a life modelled exactly on the conditions they will find in the country where they will operate. They wear Western clothing, smoke Western cigarettes, eat and drink Western foods and are served up with a constant bombardment of Western newspapers, magazines and radio and television programmes. The only language spoken by the trainees and their instructors will be that of the country into which they will be infiltrated. As well as absorbing all this background, the agents will have to learn thoroughly the deep cover stories which will have been prepared for them and to learn to respond naturally to questions in both ordinary conversation and under interrogation. This training can last for up to five years.

The 5th and 6th Directorates, Operational and Electronic, report directly to the Director of the GRU, not his deputy, as does the unnumbered Cosmic Intelligence Directorate. The 5th is larger than the first four Directorates put together and is responsible for collating reports from GRU headquarters in all sixteen military districts and from the four Fleets. It also controls Spetsnaz. The 6th Directorate is the equivalent of America's National Security Agency or Britain's GCHQ but is not an independent organization even though its functions are the same.

Having *acquired* this vast amount of intelligence from so many different sources, it then, of course, has to be analysed and interpreted, for raw data is effectively useless on its own. Thus, the 7th GRU Directorate is responsible for processing all the daily flow of information about NATO and other countries, troop, ship and aircraft movements, exercises and manoeuvres, etc. The 8th Directorate is concerned with general knowledge about the world at large, economic and political as well as purely military, and is responsible for collating biographies and personality charts of leading military and political figures.

The 9th's role is assessing new military technology as it appears, both from information published publicly as well as that gleaned or stolen by agents. The GRU regards this as one of its principal functions and the 9th Directorate therefore works very closely with the Soviet armaments industry and the Military Industrial Commission (VPK). The latter provides much of the funding which makes the GRU's gross budget larger than that of the KGB despite the fact that the GRU only employs some 25,000 people (excluding Spetsnaz) compared with the KGB's 400,000.

The 10th Directorate is concerned with military economics – production capabilities, supplies of raw materials, arms trading and the like, while the 11th studies nuclear weapons and strategies worldwide. There is said to be a 12th Directorate but we have been unable to ascertain its function, although it seems probable that it is concerned with military technology in space. There are other, unnumbered, GRU Directorates analogous to the accounts, personnel, market research and administration offices in a company, and these provide funds, passports and other documents for agents and illegals. Finally, and most secret of all, there is the GRU codes and ciphers unit, known simply as Department 8.

Notes Chapter Three

[1] In which 14,500 Polish officers were brutally murdered. Their mass graves were discovered by German troops in 1943.

[2] The Soviet Union classifies its spies as 'legals', 'illegals' and 'agents'. A 'legal' is an accredited official at an overseas embassy or consulate and enjoys diplomatic immunity, meaning that if he (or she) is detected while engaged in some spying activity, he can only be deported, not arrested and questioned. 'Illegals' are Soviet spies operating clandestinely under a cover identity, while 'agents' are foreign nationals motivated by idealism, greed, love or blackmail into spying for the USSR and its satellites.

[3] A fact long suspected but confirmed by the Swiss in 1983 when they arrested and expelled Novosti journalist Alexei Dumov and closed down the Soviet press office in Berne. Dumov admitted that his main task was to penetrate and influence Western peace movements.

[4] Formerly the province of Department 7, these four countries were re-allocated so that more time could be devoted to India and Japan in particular.

[6] Ricin is a derivative of the castor oil plant and is quoted as being twice as deadly as cobra venom, so much so that a single gramme could kill 36,000 people, suitably administered. The Markov affair is one of the best documented SovBloc assassinations. He was a Bulgarian emigré working for the BBC's overseas service, who was killed on his way home from work on the evening of 7 September 1978. A man in a bus queue stabbed him – by accident, as it seemed at the time – with the ferrule of his umbrella while he was walking over London's Waterloo Bridge. He fell feverish during the night and was admitted to hospital in the morning, dying three days later. An autopsy revealed a tiny platinum ball embedded in his thigh. When this was analysed by scientists at Britain's chemical and biological warfare defence establishment at Porton Down, the ricin was detected. Another emigré, Vladimir Kostov, had been similarly attacked in Paris ten days earlier but survived after three days in hospital intensive care.

[5] She committed suicide when her East German lover deserted her to flee the repercussions after his KGB controller, Yevgeny Runge, defected.

[7] In May 1988 a former GCHQ employee, 27-year-old Martin Chilvers, was convicted at Cardiff Crown Court of indecent assault on young boys – the same crime which led to the unmasking of

Prime's spying activities. Even though Chilvers has not been accused of espionage, the case refocused attention on the problem of people engaged in sensitive work whose sexual proclivities could make them targets for blackmail.

Members of the 'Willi Sanger' Battalion during an exercise in mountainous terrain.

Men of the 'Willi Sanger' Battalion check each other's equipment prior to a parachute drop.

A fully kitted-out East German paratrooper.

Top A member of one of the Soviet airborne divisions hauls in his parachute after a drop.

Above Spetsnaz conscripts training in urban warfare techniques.

The old KGB headquarters in Dzerzhinsky Square, Moscow.

Soviet naval infantry accompanied by T-62 tanks race ashore from a landing ship. There are approximately 17,500 men in these forces, comparable to Britain's Royal Marines. Half of them serve with the Pacific Fleet and the remainder are divided between the Northern, Baltic and Black Sea Fleets, each of which also has a naval Spetsnaz brigade.

Soviet submersibles may resemble this British Oceanics L5 …

… or the Skingsby Engineering Sea Dog with its cleated tracks.

A modified Russian 'Yankee' Class nuclear submarine. The large bulge behind the sail can only be a hangar, but it could house a miniature submarine as easily as a helicopter.

Swedish Rangers storm ashore from a patrol boat. It is their task to guard against Spetsnaz infiltration.

Soviet seamen cluster on the quayside at Ullapool. In the foreground are the lifeboats and inflatables used to ferry them to and from their ships.

Some seventy Russian and East Bloc ships were in Ullapool at the time of our visit. When someone is spotted photographing them, their decks are usually cleared.

The Soviet factory ship *Baltisnaya*. The large door in the stern could easily be used for trailing a towed array sonar or for launching midget submarines. Such vessels are frequently seen in the company of Russian warships.

Closely resembling an ordinary trawler, this is actually a Soviet 'Alpinist' Class intelligence-gathering vessel.

Chapter Four
Beneath enemy seas

A part from West Germany, neutral Sweden is one of the prime targets of Spetsnaz activity. Why Sweden? Because any Soviet invasion of Norway, NATO's critical northern flank, would necessarily involve moving Russian troops across Sweden in order to accomplish a virtual *fait accompli* before the West's quick reaction troops could be rushed into place. Moreover, the Kattegat is the Soviet Baltic Fleet's only access to Riga and Leningrad and exit to the North Sea, and is regularly patrolled by Swedish, Norwegian, Danish and West German ASW (Anti-Submarine Warfare) vessels. Ever since the late 1970s the Swedish Navy and Coastguard have observed Soviet submarines inside Swedish territorial waters, have discovered tracks made on the sea bed by amphibious mini-submarines, and have seen mysterious frogmen apparently surveying beach approaches. All of these incidents have been thoroughly investigated by the Royal Swedish Navy, the Geological Survey Department, the Defence Material Board and the Defence Research Institute, upon whose findings much of the following is based.

On 22 September 1982 the Press Department of the Swedish Defence Staff issued the following guardedly worded report which focused attention on the extent of the Soviet incursions, even though the USSR was not actually singled out as the 'aggressor' at this point.

'Foreign submarines are difficult to discover and attack. In many cases, especially skilled personnel and qualified equipment will be demanded. Our resources for ASW actions, especially in peacetime, are rather limited. According to the Supreme Commander Swedish Armed

65

Forces, General Lennart Ljung, our personnel has done a most deserving work in spite of rather unfavourable conditions.

'The ASW conditions in the Swedish eastern coastal area as well as in the western waters are totally different from those of the oceans, our waters being rather shallow, the bottom showing an utterly differing topography. Different water layers are at hand due to step-by-step variations in temperature, salinity and current at all depths. Depth and bottom conditions and the layers cause emitted sound waves to be reflected, dampened or give false reflections. In favourable conditions, a submarine may be detected at a distance of tenths [sic – 'tens' is meant] of kilometres while, under unfavourable conditions, the equivalent distance will often decrease to just a few hundred metres.

'The 1982 summer has seen an unusual number of reports from military as well as non-Service sources concerning submarines. Every report has been thoroughly studied. Some hundred of them have been of a character to result in an interrogation of the reporting person and also in a subsequent expert's analysis.

'In all, during the period more than fifty reports have been found to contain such facts as not to exclude the suspicion that they might stem from foreign submarines violating Swedish borders and trespassing on Swedish territory. This does not imply, however, that more than fifty single submarines have entered Swedish waters on a number of occasions. It rather indicates that a number of reports coincide in a way to further strengthen the probability of the presence of submarines.

'The following criteria have been utilized by Swedish authorities in judging the probability in the reportings of submarines: "submarine" – the presence of a submarine has been confirmed; "probable" – all signs point towards the presence of a submarine but no proof of it is available; and "possible" – certain signs indicate the presence of a submarine, but the information available is incomplete or partly contradictory to the subsequent analysis.

'The Supreme Commander Swedish Armed Forces suggests that, in the June–September period of 1982, foreign submarines have violated Swedish territorial borders as follows:

Month	Number of submarines	Area of reporting	Level of probability
June	2	Stockholm archipelago	"submarine"
	1	Northern Kvarken-Bottenviken	"probable'
	1	Sundsvall	"probable"
July	1	Stockholm northern archipelago	"probable"
August	1	Stockholm northern archipelago	"submarine"
	1-2	Stockholm northern archipelago	"submarine"

'Reports on "possibles" have not been compiled here.

'In the 1979–81 period, observations have been analysed and classified as follows: 1979 – one; 1980 – five; 1981 – four. In addition, there have been a number of "possible" submarine reports. Thus it has been established that in spite of the exclusion of half a year's time of reports [sic], the 1982 number of violations is considerably higher than each of the 1979–1981 years.

'Ever since the summer of 1980, which saw considerable submarine activity in the Stockholm southern archipelago, a notable change in submarine behaviour has been noted. They now act a great deal more provocatively and have been found to penetrate even deeper into our coastal waters than before. In 1981, the *U-137* striking ground within a military restricted area in the Blekinge archipelago forms a proof of this [see below].

'The reasons for the submarines trespassing on Swedish territory are not fully known. It is quite obvious, though, that one or more foreign power(s) have strong reasons for ordering submarines to violate Swedish borders. The reasons may be several different ones, amongst which one or several may be as follows:

'(1) If a foreign power intends to have its submarines operate in Swedish waters in time of war or wants to keep an option for it, then the appropriate planning will call for basic information concerning suitable areas and other forms of information not generally found in navigational charts and descriptions.

'Of great interest is also our defence preparations, especially so systems and installations within our ASW defence. It is no less important to obtain a general view on our ASW capacity. There might exist, too, a need for training in the Swedish archipelago waters, so unlike most other waters.

'(2) (A) foreign power(s) may consider the submarine a suitable platform to either check on our military exercises and testings of new equipment or to *deliver or retrieve personnel or equipment in coastal areas*[1].

'This summer a number of violations have taken place in close connection with Swedish military exercises. Thus, it seems natural to assume that violating submarines have been ordered to reconnoitre our exercises. On the other hand, on these occasions our maritime surveillance is better than at other times and, accordingly, we stand a far greater chance of discovering the intruders.'

Three years later the Swedish government was taking a much harder line. A Defence Staff memorandum of 20 September 1985 contains the following significant passage.

'One motive behind the submarine intrusions may obviously be intelligence gathering of Swedish defence preparations and exercises, including submarine defence activities. However, the repeated observations of large co-ordinated operations suggest that the task is not pure intelligence gathering. The Commission concludes that the submarine activities in Swedish waters *must be seen primarily as preparations for actual missions to be undertaken in case of war*. The exact nature of these preparations is not known, but a number of conceivable explanations has been presented. For example, they could be seen in connection with the wartime missions of *covert mining and/or the landing of diversionary forces* [ie, Spetsnaz] *for sabotage activities against crucial targets ...*'

What brought Soviet violations of Swedish coastal waters to the public eye was the stranding of 'Whiskey' Class submarine *U-137* on 27 October 1981 in the restricted area off Karlskrona naval base. This occurred during Swedish naval tests of a new wire-guided torpedo, and caused considerable embarrassment to the Soviet government.

The 'Whiskey' Class of submarine is now virtually obsolete in the patrol and attack roles but, being diesel-electric propelled, is far quieter in operation than any nuclear-powered boat. Clandestine reconnaissance is thus a natural task to be entrusted to the remaining vessels in the Soviet fleet. What puzzled Swedish naval investigators – who were not allowed access to the vessel's interior, although they were allowed to question its commander – was the distinct presence of nuclear radioactivity (identified as U-238) in the water surrounding it. This seemed to indicate that the Class is equipped with nuclear-tipped torpedoes and drew a strong protest from Prime Minister Thorbjön Fälldin. Another anomaly noted at the time was the presence of attachment hardpoints behind the sail ('conning tower'). Hardpoints for what? The answer has only gradually emerged. They are to secure a midget submarine.

Clear evidence of this emerged in October 1982, exactly a year after American Defense Secretary Caspar Weinberger was given a guided tour of the top secret Swedish naval base at Musko, in Hårsfjäden bay. Carved into the side of a mountain, Musko can accommodate both submarines and surface ships within deeply buried underground docks protected by blast-resistant doors. Here, three Soviet 'Whiskey' Class submarines, each acting as the mother ship for a mini-sub, were detected but the Swedish Navy was unable to apprehend them. Subsequently, on 1 July 1983 the Navy introduced new regulations which allow its warships to force foreign submarines detected in Swedish waters to surface, 'if necessary with arms'.

The Defence Staff memo of 20 September 1985 referred to earlier has this to say about the Musko incident:

'The Submarine Defence Commission which as a result of this incursion was appointed to evaluate the incursions and the motives behind them, stated that during this period [October 1982] six foreign submarines may have operated in the Stockholm archipelago. Three of these were hitherto unknown "midget submarines" with bottom-crawling capabilities. Two of the midget submarines together with a conventional submarine had penetrated the Hårsfjärden naval base area, whereas the third midget submarine had intruded into Stockholm harbour. Prints found at the bottom point to the involvement of these submarines in the operations. Despite considerable resources used against the intruders at Hårsfjärden, they proved insufficient and the submarines finally managed to escape. The Commission shares the conclusion drawn by experts that "the violations ... were made by Soviet submarines".'

The mini-sub which entered Stockholm harbour was actually chased for a whole week before it succeeded in eluding its pursuers, a long time for a small vessel. The Navy dropped depth charges over both the mini-sub and its mother ship when they refused to surface, but it is not known whether either was damaged. The submarines operating in Hårsfjärden bay were also depth-charged, but again with indeterminable results. Later, similar midget submarine tracks were found on the sea bed in the Oxelösund area, suggesting that the six vessels detected had been part of a much larger force.

Despite an intensification of its anti-submarine forces over recent years, the Swedish Navy has a particularly difficult task because of the hydrographic conditions off the Baltic coast referred to in the earlier report of September 1982. In the case of the Hårsfjärden intrusion, the midget subs were able to operate in shallow water and in channels where the surface craft found it difficult to manoeuvre. The rugged coastline and numerous islands also helped screen the intruders from sonar – as they would also do in time of war, of course. This has led to some speculation that the Russians may be reconnoitring safe anchorages in which their nuclear missile boats could hide, and this is certainly one possibility.

Sweden's coastline is heavily mined, the mines being inert until activated by remote control in time of war, and one of the reasons for the Soviet Union's use of midget subs is almost certainly to map their distribution. This is obviously essential if submarines are going to try to shelter in Swedish waters. Alternatively, the same need exists if the Soviet Union is planning some form of amphibious assault. Either way, sabotage teams would be needed to neutralize them, and Spetsnaz forces are well trained for this role. In March 1984, the Swedish opposition defence spokesman, Carl Bildt, said 'It is known that these forces [Spetsnaz] exist and one can speculate that, in the event of war, saboteurs might be landed from submarines to knock out specific defence installations before regular troops are sent in'.[2]

The indications suggest that the Soviets are using two types of midget submarine in these incursions, one the tracked variety and one a conventional design. The US Navy estimates[3] that they are between twenty and fifty feet long and carry three to seven men. The tracked submarine is believed to have a single propeller so that it can swim as well as crawl and may resemble an advanced version of the wartime German *'Elefant'* or *Seeteufel* ('Sea Devil') project. Developments of the *Seehund* ('Sea Dog') two-man midget submarine class which was first tested, ironically, in the Baltic during 1944 and used operationally in the closing months of the war as far abroad as the Thames estuary, these designs were among the vast volume of material captured by the Soviet Union when it overran Germany[4]. The Germans had experimented continuously with tracked submersibles, and the Red Army had been impressed with Panzer III tanks which had a schnorkel to supply air to the engine and crew and a commander's 'conning tower'. Originally modified for the invasion of Britain, Operation 'Sealion', which was eventually abandoned, these tanks were used to force a crossing of the River Bug in 1941 during the first day of the German advance into Russian occupied Poland.

The Soviet Union reacted positively to the idea of submersible tanks, already having a penchant (which continues to this day) for amphibious designs. The advantages of such vehicles have largely been ignored in the West, and only the Federal Republic of Germany's Leopard 1 and 2 tanks can match the capabilities of Soviet tanks and can ford rivers – or wade ashore from landing craft – at a submerged depth of four metres (13 ft).

It is generally believed that the midget subs utilize a diesel engine and battery propulsion like any conventional submarine, the diesel being fed air through a schnorkel to charge the batteries and exhausting its fumes through the same system. They may even be purely battery-driven, but the fact that one evidently survived for a week submerged while pursued by the Swedish Navy makes this unlikely. The batteries would not only have to provide propulsion but also operate the life support, lighting and heating systems, carbon dioxide scrubbers, etc. However, caterpillar tracks would demand far less energy output than a propeller. These factors taken together make one speculate – although speculation is all it can be – that these craft are actually nuclear-powered, hence the radiation in the water.

Many people have questioned why the Soviet Union should employ tracked submarines in the first place. One explanation could be that their propeller is used to get them in the general vicinity of the target, then they settle to the bottom to avoid strong coastal currents which would deter a conventional mini-sub. Apart from this, in the covert Spetsnaz role the ability to climb a beach is an obvious asset. A mini-sub could carry more equipment than a combat frogman could. If made of steel, it could serve as a rudimentary armoured personnel carrier once on land, although practical considerations make this unlikely (see below). It could also be used as an ambulance for casualties or as the 'getaway vehicle' for kidnapped VIPs in an enemy country.

The US Naval Institute[5] has this to say about Soviet use of mini-subs:

'There are many theories about the Soviet motives behind these peacetime mini-submarine intrusions into the territorial waters of other nations. They include:
> Collecting intelligence on defensive installations and navigational conditions near naval bases
> Conducting new weapons systems trials
> Observing foreign military exercises
> Inserting/extracting Spetsnaz teams or agents
> Testing adversary military capabilities, detector systems and crisis management techniques
> Laying passive navigation devices as underwater route markers to safe havens for Soviet nuclear-powered fleet ballistic missile submarines in Swedish and Norwegian fjords in the event of war
> Laying mines
> Removing mines or other underwater devices
> Locating and tapping underwater communications cables to collect intelligence or feed in false data.
'All of these theories are plausible and possibly correct, and all are in keeping with the Spetsnaz doctrinal mission of special reconnaissance.'

To evaluate the Soviet mini-subs, we approached the British company Slingsby Engineering, who are among the world leaders in underwater vehicle design and development. They manufacture midget submarines which have chambers to allow divers to 'lock in' and 'lock out' and which can also be used as deep sea submersible rescue vessels to aid the crew of a damaged submarine. Slingsby's principal interest is in designs for work related to offshore gas and oil drilling installations, one of which is called *Sea Dog!*

Sea Dog is an unmanned, remotely piloted vessel fitted with sea bed tracks, or crawlers. It is designed to bury underwater cables and is steered by an operator sitting in a surface vessel through its integral video camera and navigation system. It is not, however, free-roaming, being connected to its own 'mother ship' by means of an umbilical cable.

From the meagre information about Soviet tracked mini-subs we were able to supply him, Slingsby's Senior Design Engineer, Paul Clapham, helpfully supplied the following data, although it must be clearly understood that this is 'intelligent guesswork', not confirmed fact.

'It has been assumed', he said, 'that the Soviet vehicles are approximately equal to the LR4 and LR5 [Slingsby manned submersibles]. These can carry up to five people. The energy required to drive a tracked vehicle *in water* of this size at one knot would require between 150 and 300 Kilowatt Hours, which is between 2½ and five times the battery capacity of the LR types.

'The addition of batteries would add between ten and twenty tonnes to the overall air weight, which then becomes relevant. We set a depth rating of a hundred feet of sea water on the vehicle, which reduces the pressure hull weight to compensate for the life support system and the tracks. We now have a vehicle weighing, out of water, some 35-40 tonnes, with dimensions of approximately ten metres long by four high and four wide.

'The vehicle would have the ability to become neutrally buoyant for its transition to and from sea bed to parent submarine. This causes no problem and is controlled by taking on and pumping out ballast water. This can also be used to reduce the weight of the tracks on the sea bed. Perhaps the most interesting point here is that in water the vehicle can carry sufficient power, but for it to crawl up on to a beach, batteries are driving a vehicle weighing between 35 and 40 tonnes.

'Possible reasons for the use of track systems would be to reduce the motive energy required to drive the vehicle: contact by tracks with the sea bed is considered to be almost a hundred per cent efficient, whilst a propeller system is only sixty per cent. The tracked system would allow considerably more control in confined areas, especially so if cross-currents were encountered.'

Although it appears from this that the vehicle is precluded from moving ashore, it could nevertheless go very close to a beach, certainly close enough to be of value to covert operations, delivering stores or personnel ashore, or spiriting Spetsnaz teams and captured VIPs away.

Life support has been calculated on experience gained with the LR class of boats, which have an eight-hour mission and three-day emergency backup system. Postulating a vehicle in the 30-40 tonne class could increase that considerably. The Soviets have extensive experience in space and will undoubtedly have extended that knowledge to miniature submarine systems.

It would be interesting to know what sort of caterpillar tracks the Russians use. If they are of tank or armoured personnel carrier type, they will require a great deal of maintenance to ensure reliability. On the other hand, they may be of the type developed for *Sea Dog* which comprise a reinforced rubber conveyor belt with aluminium grousers bolted on to aid traction.

Nor is Sweden itself the sole target for these nautical incursions. Soviet submarines are very active off the Norwegian coast and midget submarine tracks have been spotted in Japan's Soya and Tsugaru Straits (August 1984) as well as in the vicinity of offshore rigs in the North Sea. (These are classed as strategic targets because denying oil to an enemy is one potent means of strangling his mobility.) The Soviets' main problem, though, is access to the world's oceans without tripping the numerous underwater sound, heat and electrical detection systems lying on the sea bed which serve as a 'burglar alarm' for the West, particularly in the critical Greenland-Iceland-UK (GIUK) Gap and around the shores of Japan. Hence the additional focus on Norway, where Hardangerfjord is a major centre in NATO's underwater Sound Surveillance System (SOSUS). Another bottleneck for the Soviet Navy is Gibraltar, and similar underwater track marks have been observed on the sea bed after large Soviet fishing factory ships have passed through the Straits. Russian merchant ships of all shapes and sizes are also involved in another aspect of Spetsnaz activity, as we shall see.

Submarines and mini-subs are not the only means Spetsnaz uses to reconnoitre enemy or potential enemy shores.

5 March 1984, Stockholm (Reuter). 'Swedish troops hunting a foreign submarine fired at frogmen seen emerging from the sea yesterday on the tiny island of Almoe.'

Since the 1950s, the Soviet Union has expended a great deal of energy and money in developing elite combat swimmer/ diver units comparable to those of the US Sea/Air/Land (SEAL) teams and the British Special Boat Squadron. At the end of the Second World War, the USSR lacked knowledge in this specialist area, its main conflict against Germany having been on the land, and one of the most remarkable stories connected with the creation of Soviet combat frogman units is that of Royal Navy Commander Lionel 'Buster' Crabb. Crabb was a war hero and an experienced diver who in the post-war period was frequently employed by British intelligence. Mike and Jackie Welham have researched the macabre story of Crabb's disappearance in Portsmouth harbour in 1956, during the visit to Britain of the Soviet cruiser *Ordzohnikidze*, and through new evidence to be published in a forthcoming book[6] have come to the following conclusions.

1) That Crabb was involved in an undercover mission involving MI6 and the CIA but that the Russians were tipped off by a mole within British intelligence – possibly Sir Roger Hollis – and captured him.

2) That the headless and handless body of a diver which was later found in a semi-decomposed state was not Crabb's, as was generally assumed at the time, but a 'plant', the corpse of a man of similar stature deliberately left in the sea where the tides and currents would bring it ashore. Moreover, that key witnesses were intimidated into silence or perjury at the inquest, which was itself rigged to draw only one conclusion.

3) That Crabb was taken to Russia and given the choice of execution as a spy or of co-operating with the Soviet Navy.

4) That he was for several years actively involved at a naval training school on the Black Sea created in the year of his disappearance by Rear Admiral A. Kisov, helping the Soviet Navy develop modern sub-aqua techniques and equipment.

5) That he died only a few years ago in Czechoslovakia.

Certainly, it is now known that each of the four Soviet Fleets each has a Spetsnaz Brigade of similar size to the Army units. The US Navy[7] gives their composition as a headquarters company, a battalion specially trained in parachuting into water, a mini-submarine group, two to three combat swimmer battalions and a signals company. They wear the uniforms of ordinary naval infantry and, as in the Army, their very existence is unknown to the average Russian sailor. They are trained for exactly the same tasks as their airborne colleagues but would infiltrate their objectives from the sea or up rivers.

As related in Mike Welham's other forthcoming book, on the subject of modern combat frogmen (also to be published by Patrick Stephens Ltd), the first glimpse the West had of Spetsnaz frogmen came on 27 September 1983. A message arrived in the office of Sweden's Coastal Defence Group at Vaxholm that an observer at a defence station on Stockholm's northern sector had observed unidentified combat swimmers on an island close to the station. Reaction was immediate: police, coast guard and military forces were alerted and ships and helicopters swiftly despatched to the area. After a long search, however, they were unable to find any trace of the intruders, or of the submarine which must have brought them close to the coast.

The man who had spotted the swimmers was questioned intensively, for his evidence was critical. He had travelled from his island home to the mine control station on another island, using a small boat. After landing, at about 10.30 on a fine, clear morning, he was making his way to his post when he saw something in the water, some distance off the beach. At first he thought it was a seal, for they are quite common in the Baltic. To get a better view, he climbed on to the roof of a building, and from this vantage point could see clearly that it was not a seal but a man. He then spotted a second swimmer, and finally a third man crouched on the beach amidst some rocks. The three men were in line.

In his testimony, he estimated that the furthest swimmer was about a hundred metres offshore, and said that the three men were roped together. Only the man on the beach could be described in any detail. He was dressed in a black diving suit and had two cylinders on his back with two hoses going to his mouthpiece. It was later determined that this must have been of the closed circuit 'rebreather' type used almost exclusively by military divers because it emits no tell-tale bubbles to reveal an underwater swimmer's presence.

The Swedish observer climbed down from the roof and started walking back towards the beach, at which point the diver on the shore waded unhurriedly back into the water.

The three frogmen then submerged and disappeared from view. To begin with the observer thought the divers must be part of the Swedish Navy's 'Rangers', but when they failed to reappear after some time he decided to put out an alarm.

The man was questioned by SÄPO, the Swedish security police, who are highly skilled in detecting lies or anomalies in witnesses' statements, and they accepted his evidence as factual. He had been a serving officer since 1970 and was a trusted guard and reliable observer.

What concerned the authorities was what these divers were doing so close to the mine defence station, one of the posts from which the mines off the coast would be activated in time of war. The post is a particularly important one, controlling a channel leading into Stockholm harbour. The building itself is built of rock and concrete and oversees a stretch of water which is freely used by merchant shipping but in which diving is prohibited because of the possibility of one of the mines being detonated by accident. The channel floor is also laid with cables connecting the mines and with underwater sound detectors. The obvious conclusion drawn by the Swedish authorities was that the three men were engaged in reconnoitring the inshore defences and using the rope connecting them to measure distances. This is just the sort of work for which naval Spetsnaz units are specifically trained.

Six months later, on Saturday, 3 March 1984, there was an even more dramatic incident in which Swedish forces fired on unidentified divers, this time in the vicinity of Karlskrona naval base. The Swedish Navy had been hunting an elusive submarine for three weeks, and was on the alert for both a mini-sub and its parent vessel. As a result, ground forces were also deployed, scouring the coastline with tracker dogs. Late in the Saturday evening a number of frogmen were spotted on the shore of Almoe island and, after ascertaining that there were no Swedish divers in the area, permission was obtained to open fire. No casualties were observed and the frogmen disappeared beneath the waves without making any attempt to shoot back. Amazingly, swimmers were seen again in the dim light of the following dawn, and the Swedish troops opened up again but without seemingly hitting anyone.

Reinforcements were called in and an intensive sweep made of the area. At one point, the army halted a funeral procession and, after checking the identity of each of the mourners, even insisted that the coffin be opened to check that there was not a frogman inside! Despite this search, no-one was apprehended.

One theory[8] is that the swimmers were from a midget submarine which they had been forced to evacuate after such a prolonged underwater vigil. They would then have tried to lay up out of sight before making a rendezvous with their mother ship. Another possibility is that they were on a deliberate reconnaissance mission. Whatever the truth, they disappeared without trace, and no submarine was physically discovered.

Karlskrona is a natural target for Spetsnaz, because it is not only one of Sweden's major naval shipyards but also headquarters of the coastal artillery, which is responsible for the defence of Sweden's coastline. Similar importance is attached to Subic Bay in the Philippines, on the other side of the world. This is a major US Navy base which has seen at least one similar incursion. Although the Navy has not released any details, it has denied suggestions that the intruders were Philippine insurgents 'because of the sophistication of the equipment and the professionalism of the operatives'.

Spetsnaz also seems to be flexing its muscles in Alaska. 'Soviet forces "invade" US island off Alaska', said *The Daily Telegraph* on 12 February 1988. 'Are Russians using Alaska?' asked *The Herald Tribune* on the same day.

Alaska, of course, used to belong to Russia before the United States purchased it in 1867 for $7,200,000 – a deal which, although perfectly legal, has quietly infuriated the Soviet Union ever since it came into existence, especially because of the 49th State's mineral riches. Some 450,000 square miles make up some of the most inhospitable land on the Earth. The landscape is bleak and rugged, the weather harsh, transportation limited and the coastline usually icebound, but Alaska is a prime source of that vital strategic mineral, oil. It is today also part of the American front line as vital as Norway, Britain or West Germany, and hosts much of the West's most sophisticated early warning and air and sea defence systems.

On the ground, the first line of defence lies with the Alaska Eskimo Scout Battalions. These men, amongst the elite forces of the world although 'only' a National Guard formation, are eskimaux or indian, brought up in the wild and thoroughly acclimatized to the land and the weather. There are three Alaska battalions, each of six companies, but the principal scouting unit is a team of five men – a Sergeant team leader, a radio operator, and three scouts. In this they parallel the operational set-up of special forces world-wide. These teams are located in 63 towns and villages throughout Alaska, and each man has a regular job in addition to serving as a scout. He keeps his uniform and weapons at home but is on constant call-out. Born and bred to the terrain, he is familiar with all its perils and tricks and will spot any anomaly, such as footprints in the snow where none should exist. Any such sightings are immediately radioed to Fort Richardson, headquarters of USARAL (US Army Reserve Alaska). Key locations on which the Alaskan Scouts focus attention are St Lawrence Island, the Pribilofs and Little Diomede, the latter lying only three miles from Big Diomede, which is part of the USSR and houses a military detachment.

On 12 February 1988 Dean Fosdick of Associated Press reported that:

'Soviet commandos may be staging covert landings on a United States island in the Bering Sea. American officials say Soviet military gear has been found after sightings of mysterious strangers running away.

'An increasing number of reports of unidentified aircraft, submarines, swimmers in scuba gear and discarded military equipment are being made to US intelligence agencies.'

On the same day United Press International reported that Scout patrols on St Lawrence Island 'have found Soviet-made military gear, including a gas mask and buoys with explosive charges'.

The Pentagon plays down such reports, dismissing the evidence as discarded material which happened to be washed ashore. Two miles inland[9]? If similar occurrences have been noticed in England, they have been promptly hushed up, the Official Secrets Act being generally respected by the British media. But ...

Notes Chapter Four

[1] Our italics.

[2] *The Daily Telegraph*, 7 March 1984.

[3] *Proceedings*, August 1987.

[4] *The Illustrated Encyclopaedia of 20th Century Weapons and Warfare*, Purnell, 1967-69 and Phoebus/BPC, 1971-78.

[5] *Proceedings*, August 1987.

[6] Published by Columbus Books, 1989.

[7] *Proceedings*, August 1987.

[8] *Baltimore Sun*, 5 March 1984.

[9] *International Herald Tribune*, 12 February 1988.

Chapter Five
Fishing expeditions

A great deal of concern has been growing over recent years at the presence of dozens of Russian and Warsaw Pact fishing vessels in British and Scottish ports close to sensitive military installations. Newspaper speculation first brought the subject into the public eye, but more recently both senior naval officers and Home Office officials have confirmed that a problem does exist and belated measures are now being put in hand to help control the situation – a situation in which some 35,000 Soviet Bloc seamen each year are free to wander more or less where they will and even to visit modern Royal Navy warships during Open Days.

'Klondyker fleet swells to 41 ships', declared the *Aberdeen Press and Journal* on 16 October 1985; 'MP calls for Ullapool "spies" probe' (5 November 1985); 'Blue Toon set for Red fleet invasion' (2 August 1986); 'Mackerel gives food for thought' (24 October 1986); 'Klondyker days set to end' (15 January 1987). Purely a local concern ...? Hardly. *The Daily Express*, 14 April 1987: 'Navy in move to curb menace of Soviet spy ships', said Defence Correspondent Peter Hitchens; 'Russian sailors roam Britain', echoed former *Daily Telegraph* Naval Correspondent Desmond Wettern.

'Klondyker' is the term the press has adopted to call Soviet and Warsaw Pact fishing vessels, harking back to the days of the Klondike gold rush in north-west Canada in the 1890s. Today, fish are in some ways more precious than gold to a Russian population always hovering on the brink of famine, and the size of the Soviet fishing fleet is constantly expanding. Moreover, when their vessels are unsuccessful in filling their holds with sufficient herring or mackerel, Soviet Masters will purchase fish from British and European locals, and have become welcome customers in many harbours. The fact that their crewmen do not stride down the streets wearing jackboots and fur caps festooned with the hammer and sickle, but instead spend good money buying radios, hi-fis and other consumer goods scarce in Russia and then return aboard without getting drunk and smashing up the local pubs and hotels, has a disarming effect on the local populace who tend to dismiss as nonsense any suggestion that such men could be involved in espionage or sabotage.

Merchant seamen of any nationality are free to walk ashore in most Western ports during their off-duty hours and do not even need a passport – an international seaman's card and contract of employment is sufficient proof of identity[1]. Western seamen in *Russian* ports are, however, restricted to the harbour area itself and cannot wander off sightseeing at will. Desmond Wettern said that the British government had been warned 'by senior intelligence officers' of the danger of Russian sailors 'entering Britain freely each year', and that British intelligence is 'said to be alarmed by the Government's inaction'.

In November 1985 Mr Tony Baldry, Conservative MP for Banbury, asked the Government to reveal how many people came ashore from Warsaw Pact ships at the ports of Ullapool, Aberdeen, Stornoway and Leith. In the same month, the SDP MP for Ross, Cromarty and Skye, Mr Charles Kennedy, asked Home Secretary Mr Douglas Hurd if there were plans to prevent Soviet agents entering Britain at Ullapool. Further concern was expressed by the Secretary of the Customs and Excise group of the Society of Civil and Public Servants. Interviewed on BBC television, Mr Tony Lewis claimed that understaffing meant that immigration and customs officers were unable to keep check on Soviet sailors coming ashore. Replying to Mr Baldry's question, Home Office spokesman Mr David Waddington said that crew members of all nationalities were normally exempt from having to obtain formal permission from immigration officers to go ashore. 'They are required to leave the port with their ship,' he continued, and 'the Master is required to provide a crew list and to report any deserter.' Significantly, he added, 'Records are not kept of seamen coming ashore in this way'. Mr Waddington refused to disclose details of what checks are made on foreign seamen entering Britain.

Mr Baldry said in a subsequent interview that 'If the Soviet authorities wanted to get Soviet personnel into this country, all they would have to do is simply let them off at Ullapool, Aberdeen, or anywhere else. The Captain would be a party to that plan and simply would not report them missing. We have no idea who comes into the country in these circumstances, and that is a matter of very great concern.'

In the *Daily Express*, Peter Hitchens said that 'The growing danger was revealed yesterday by Admiral Sir Nicholas Hunt, NATO's Commander in Chief for the Eastern Atlantic. He said the Communist bloc almost certainly includes its merchant fleet in its war plans.

'The navy suspects that at the outbreak of war the trading vessels would quickly abandon their peacetime guise and lay mines, drop saboteurs ashore or scuttle themselves in harbour mouths and sea lanes.

'Every day, 73 Communist merchant vessels are in NATO ports, more than one third of them targeted on Britain.'

To which Desmond Wettern added, 'Every Russian foreign-going merchant ship has at least one KGB officer on board. Russian naval officers regularly go to sea as merchant seamen to gain intelligence.' One of the reasons the British Government extended the territorial limit from three to twelve miles on 1 October 1987 was to prevent Soviet spy trawlers[2] monitoring Polaris nuclear submarine arrivals and departures from Faslane, their base in the Firth of Clyde.

One of the Scottish ports regularly used by Soviet fishing vessels and factory ships which gives British security concern is Peterhead, on the east coast of Scotland. To its south, alongside the main road to Aberdeen, lies RAF Buchan, whose massive green radomes advertise the presence of Highland Radar. This installation is a vital part of Britain's defences, being the air defence and warning centre for the northern sector. And although the heart of the installation is buried deep underground, the radomes themselves are extremely vulnerable to sabotage. Buchan fulfils dual roles as a command post and a reporting centre, and is one of four such installations in the UK. However, it is the closest to the area from which any Soviet aerial attack would probably come.

If an unidentified aircraft enters Scottish airspace it is RAF Buchan which instigates the Quick Reaction Alert (QRA) and directs scrambled interceptors on to the intruder. It will also guide and control the in-flight refuelling tankers which are needed to keep the fighters in the air.

Following the coast northwards from Peterhead around into the Moray Firth you come to RAF Kinloss, home to maritime surveillance Nimrod aircraft as well as Buccaneers and Jaguars. This would be another obvious target for Soviet sabotage teams in time of war. There is another, though slightly less sensitive, command and reporting centre at Benbecula, on the Isle of Uist, off the north-west coast. The RAF also has a forward operating base at Stornoway, on the Isle of Lewis. Both of these are within easy reach of Ullapool, another haven for Russian and Eastern Bloc fishing vessels. Further south, the nuclear submarine base at Faslane is obviously a prime target for an enemy, but Glasgow airport and Macrihanish would also both handle military traffic in time of war. In the far north, another command and reporting post is situated on Unst in the Shetland Isles, while the airfield at Sumburgh has been modernized and would be available to NATO aircraft in the event of hostilities. Speculation that the latest American 'stealth' aircraft may be based in Scotland will obviously spur further Soviet interest.

Each of the above installations is a potential target for Spetsnaz teams, and what better way to scout them out than under the guise of innocent merchant seamen? But theory is all very well. Is there any *evidence*?

28 August 1986. Mike Welham was in Peterhead. The day was overcast and no fewer than seven large Soviet fishing factory ships were moored in the harbour confines. For the people of the port, they are welcome visitors, bringing extra trade to both local fishermen and to the shops in the town. Lifeboats and black rubber inflatable launches ferried constantly between them.

One vessel, the *Sovetskya Latvia*, was moored against the northern breakwater, and could be examined more closely than the other ships. Vessels of this type are around 16,000 tons displacement, have a crew complement of around 260 and boast a cinema, sauna and helipad which can be used for games of football or volleyball. In common with all the other ships, the vessel was fairly old, its grey hull and dirty white upperworks faded and weathered. Such ships are away from their home ports for half of each year and maintaining appearances takes a low priority. The *Sovetskya Latvia* had two holds, divided by a central superstructure housing the bridge and surmounted by the helipad, which was shrouded by a net.

During his four-day stay in Peterhead, Mike was accompanied by Graham Sykes, a local man with no military background who was able to act as an independent witness with no axe to grind. He did not know the purpose of Mike's visit to the port until he was told afterwards. The pair walked up and down the breakwater several times each day, and watched the other vessels through binoculars.

A guard was stationed on the gangplank at all times, his right hand permanently in the pocket of his black reefer jacket. Armed guards are posted on all Soviet ships in foreign ports as much to prevent unauthorized crew members leaving the vessel as to stop uninvited visitors. Even in August, the guards wore fur hats. Each had an orange armband.

In the forward well area men loaded barrels into a net and transferred the load into a smaller vessel moored alongside. Other men were assembling barrels. All perfectly normal activity. The men – and women – aboard were generally as unkempt as the ship itself, typical hardworking seamen. Compared with the local Scottish fishermen, though, they seemed humourless. One never saw a smile and all conversation seemed directed at the work in hand. The contrast was all the greater therefore, when one morning a door opened in the upperworks and a woman of altogether different character appeared. A trim brunette with well groomed hair, wearing makeup and dressed in a grey/brown suit and semi high-heeled shoes, she was a complete contrast to the rest of the crew. When she saw Mike and Graham watching her, she promptly re-entered the door. Master's wife? Ship's secretary? Doctor? Or security officer? When they asked the ship's captain about her, Mike and Graham were told no such woman existed.

When crewmen ventured ashore, it was noticeable that they always went in groups, never alone. Unlike Western seamen, they did not head straight for the nearest pub, but seemed totally intent on spending their hard-earned wages on radio-cassette players and television sets. Defection from Soviet merchant vessels is extremely rare, for each man knows his wife, girlfriend or family stands hostage for his good behaviour while abroad.

Mike began to think he was on a wild goose chase in Peterhead until the third morning when, strolling past the ship with Graham for the umpteenth time, he noticed a group of men exercising on the upper deck. There were fifteen to twenty of them, partially obscured by the lifeboats, but it was immediately apparent that they were in a totally different category to the rest of the crew. Short-haired and wearing PT vests and track suit trousers, they were vigorously exercising with dumb-bells. Graham observed that they seemed to be taking their exercise very seriously. Moreover, you would not normally expect a group of keep-fit enthusiasts to be dressed so uniformly. Graham commented afterwards that he was 'physically stunned', for even his inexperienced eye knew that what he saw was not normal.

Another man now appeared on the deck, saw the direction of Mike's and Graham's gaze, and waved the athletes below. He then reappeared with a camera and photographed the pair on the breakwater. Something else for KGB or GRU files, without a shadow of doubt.

Afterwards, Mike asked Graham for his impressions. He commented that the men looked like a military team.

Next day they were on deck again, kicking a ball about on the helipad. A ship's officer spoke to them, and moments later a pair of them appeared at the head of the gangway. The guard, who normally checked the other seamen as they went ashore, ignored them, nor did the men speak to him. They were dressed in the same PT kit as on the previous morning. To Mike and Graham's trepidation, the men appeared to be making straight towards them ... but walked past. They were of athletic build and had a military bearing, plus, as Graham said, 'cold, dark eyes'. The men walked to the steps leading down to the water where they met a lifeboat from one of the other ships. A package was passed to them and they returned to the *Sovetskya Latvia*.

Graham was visibly shaken by the encounter, even more so when Mike later showed him a magazine article on Spetsnaz. Even with his limited knowledge he could see how such men could well be spies or saboteurs, and even mentioned the nearby presence of RAF Buchan, even though he did not know what function the base serves.

While at Peterhead Mike and Graham also observed a cluster of East German trawlers moored in the middle of the harbour, well away from casual inspection. They were all painted matt black, which gave them a sinister appearance when contrasted with the gaily painted Scottish fishing boats. Mike and Graham spent several hours watching them, and not once saw a single crewman on deck. The only indication of life was when lights came on in the evening. When the trawlers departed, they did so in single file and with regular spacing, for all the world like a naval convoy.

Another piece of rather more speculative evidence which was brought to our attention during Mike's trip to Scotland was a strange story told him by a local fisherman who asked quite forcibly to remain anonymous when Mike explained the reason for his interest. He said he had been idly gazing out across the harbour one evening when he saw what appeared to be a small boat. There was nothing unusual about this, but it had appeared quite suddenly from nowhere. It moved slowly towards the shore and then, as mysteriously as it had appeared, it vanished from sight again. The man said his immediate thought was that it had sunk, but he did not know how to report a boat which came from nowhere and then vanished again. Mike asked him whether it could have been a submarine, but the man said it was too small. Could it, however, have been a midget sub similar to those whose track marks have been seen on the sea-floor close to offshore rigs?

* * *

Security in naval dockyards, not just in Britain but in other member countries of NATO, is often a farce, for on open days members of the public are allowed to wander with almost total freedom around modern warships, including nuclear-powered attack submarines (but not missile boats). The only parts of the ships normally sealed off from inspection are the communications departments with their coding and enciphering equipment, but the control centres and weapon departments can be examined, although not photographed.

Even without photography, a trained observer who knows what he or she is looking for can record a number of valuable impressions, and concealed miniature cameras are a distinct possibility for visitors to the ships are not subjected even to the most cursory search. Similarly, though certain areas of dockyards are sealed off for most of the year, they can be examined and measured on these open days in more detail than can be achieved by satellite photography. With Soviet and Warsaw Pact seamen having the freedom to wander where they will, it is a certainty that among the thousands of innocent visitors there will be a number of GRU specialists, who may include members of Spetsnaz. And what about some of these attractive girls coming on board? Could one be looking for a lonely sailor who might boast about his work after she had bestowed her favours on him? The 'swallow' form of intelligence gathering, as we have already seen, is a favourite Soviet trick.

Britain is not the only country which holds open Navy Days. On Sunday, 29 May 1988, warships of the Dutch Navy were on view in Amsterdam. They included an anti-submarine frigate and a mine hunter, while a PAP 104 remote-controlled underwater search vehicle was also on display. Moored close by was the Soviet cruise vessel *Leonid Brezhnev*, and many of the visitors aboard the Dutch ships were of Eastern Bloc nationalities. They will undoubtedly have included GRU and/or naval Spetsnaz personnel amongst their numbers. (The Soviet Navy holds open days too, but never when a Western vessel is scheduled to be in port!)

Rotterdam's Europort has become the Soviet Union's main trading centre in Western Europe over recent years, and today Warsaw Pact ships and trucks almost overflow the port. The Soviet government originally wanted to establish its own import/export agencies staffed by Russian personnel in Rotterdam, a proposal which was initially rejected by the Dutch government. When the SovBloc nations retaliated by boycotting the port, the loss of revenue to the Netherlands caused a rapid change of mind. The result is that Rotterdam is now a key centre for Warsaw Pact activity in the West, and harbour officials have told us that the Soviet agency offices carry twice the staff they need. When this fact is coupled to the knowledge that every Soviet merchant ship forms part of the naval reserve and that each carries at least one KGB or GRU officer aboard, some obvious conclusions can be drawn.

In his book *A Crime Against The World*[3], defector Vladil Lysenko, a former fishing boat Captain, observes that the Soviet fishing fleet and merchant marine are constantly engaged in operations which have nothing to do with commerce and the peaceful functions indicated by their names, and are intensively utilized for military and intelligence-gathering purposes. The Soviet fishing fleet, he says, is maintained in a permanent state of readiness for total mobilization on a war footing. All Soviet merchant and fishing craft are, by design, semi-naval vessels, and all their crews are obliged to undergo naval training. In the Captain's safe aboard every Soviet ship is a sealed packet of instructions to be followed in the event of the outbreak of war, to be opened only upon receipt of a coded radio signal.

'Not infrequently', Lysenko writes, 'parties of professional naval intelligence officers, usually four or five of
them, are assigned to sail aboard fishing vessels. On two
occasions I sailed out of Murmansk with naval intelligence
officers on board. It began when I was summoned to the
representative of naval intelligence, a Captain. He said:
"Some extra men will be sailing with you. You are the
Captain, a trusted officer, and I am to tell you they are five
officers of naval intelligence. Prepare their quarters!"

'On a deepwater trawler, as a rule, the working quarters
allotted to an intelligence team are the small sick bay plus a
little extra cabin in the upper deck superstructure
immediately abaft the bridge. Two days before we were due
to sail, the officers arrived wearing naval uniform – reefer
tunics, epaulettes, gold braid: two Junior Lieutenants
under the command of a Senior Lieutenant. Then some
navy trucks drove up loaded with several large wooden
boxes of equipment, which were carried aboard by naval
bluejackets and installed in their quarters, after which the
former sick bay was declared out of bounds to everyone else,
including me. The officers began to set up their apparatus,
and it was impossible to conceal the fact that they were
planting an absolute forest of aerials of all types on top of
the superstructure: parabolic, directional, T-shaped, VHF
and long-range aerials.

'Apart from their radio equipment, the naval intelligence
party also had cameras fitted with long, powerful telephoto
lenses, with which they took photos through the ship's
portholes. One day an American nuclear submarine passed
close by us, sailing on the surface. On seeing the submarine,
our intelligence boys could not resist the temptation to
come out on deck, and without bothering to conceal
themselves either from us or from the Americans, began
snapping away from all angles with their telephoto lenses.

'Soviet fishing vessels are also obliged to render all
possible aid and co-operation to auxiliary vessels of the
Soviet Navy, which are constantly stationed off the North
American coast[4], either engaged in intelligence work or
servicing Soviet submarines. These auxiliary vessels are
usually MFTs[5] of the 'Ocean' type, built in East Germany
and commissioned into the Soviet Navy almost as soon as

delivered. Not far from Severomorsk – the main base of the Soviet Northern Fleet – these vessels have their own special base, where at least twenty of them (excluding those at sea) are always to be found moored up. They are painted in the usual colours of the Soviet fishing fleet, but are completely under naval control and wholly manned by naval seamen wearing civilian clothes.'

Rotterdam is an ideal location for KGB and GRU personnel and houses the KGB Western European depot, one of whose more unusual functions over the years has, according to Desmond Wettern, been the distribution of hard pornography, presumably to help undermine Western cultural values. The port sees extensive NATO ship movements, and it is no coincidence that whenever a Western warship is taking on stores, a Warsaw Pact vessel will be seen nearby. Mechanical 'breakdowns' are frequently given as excuses for Warsaw Pact vessels overstaying in Western ports where any military activity can be observed. During one visit to Rotterdam, Mike observed a Dutch submarine in drydock for a refit. Despite the presence of a Kon Marechaussee, or marine security police, launch close by, there was nothing to prevent photographs being taken from a Soviet merchant ship moored at the wharf unloading and loading. The same often happens in Hull, where British diesel-electric attack submarines undergo repairs and refits.

On another occasion Mike spoke to a Dutch diving supervisor who has extensive experience of Soviet ships in Rotterdam. He is employed by a company which contracts to clean the hulls of ships while they are loading or waiting for a berth. This requires divers to guide rotating scouring brushes over the hull bottom, removing marine growth and thereby saving valuable drydocking time and money.

The diving supervisor told Mike of one singular occasion when his company had been hired by an agent to clean the hull of a Soviet bulk carrier – in itself, not an uncommon occurrence. The diving team motored in a small boat out to the Soviet vessel and tied up at the ladder, for it is normal practice for the supervisor to speak to the ship's Captain before commencing work. Accompanied by another diver, the supervisor climbed the ladder to be greeted at the top by three unsmiling men armed with sub-machine-guns, later identi- fied as Skorpions[6]. He was asked abruptly what he wanted and when he explained was ordered to accompany two of the men while the third remained on guard at the head of the ladder.

In the Captain's cabin, the supervisor was again asked what he wanted. When he explained, the Captain demanded to know who had sent him. He gave the agent's name and the Captain telephoned, speaking rapidly in Russian. As the Captain raised his voice, the supervisor guessed that he had not been notified of the arrangement. Finally the Captain replaced the 'phone and gave him a hard look. He told the supervisor to carry on, but that on no account was any member of his team to board the ship again. He snapped an order at the two guards who escorted the bewildered supervisor back to the ladder. Throughout the time the diving team was working, they were at all times watched by two armed men.

Under the hull, which was heavily encrusted with barnacles, the divers noticed two things not normal on a merchant vessel. Apart from a hole in the forward part of the hull through which a standard depth ranging sonar could be lowered, there was a much larger hole through which far more sophisticated equipment could be lowered. There was also a large fixed sonar dome, approximately a metre in diameter, identified as a naval type. The supervisor also told Mike that the ship was fitted with heavy duty cranes which could be moved independently, which is again unusual for a vessel of this type. He volunteered the opinion that the ship would be ideal for submarine support operations and that the cranes could easily lift midget submarines stowed in the vessel's capacious holds.

Apart from merchant vessels and spy trawlers, Soviet research vessels play an important role in the overall intelligence gathering operation. As well as genuine oceanographic and meteorological research equipment, they are festooned with electronic detection and surveillance antennae and radomes. Some also carry towed sonar arrays[7], and deep sea submersibles which could be used for submarine rescue duties or for transporting divers inshore. Since the Territorial Waters Act of 1987, they have been unable to linger as close to the coastline of the British Isles as before, but they are still present. A recent development of concern to British naval security is the agreement signed in May 1988 between the Irish and Russian governments to undertake a joint underwater survey to assess the deep water species of fish around the Irish coast and into the Atlantic. The agreement also gives the Soviet vessels access to Irish shore facilities, and as Bernard Moffatt of the Celtic League in the Isle of Man told us, there is a very fine line between 'research' and 'intelligence'. Indeed, the first two Russian vessels to visit Dublin were 'Alpinist' Class AGIs.

One reason this agreement will have delighted the GRU is that the Royal Navy has largely stopped sending its submarines from Faslane out into the Atlantic through the narrow gap between the Mull of Kintyre and Rathlin island, off the north coast of Ireland, but instead routes them south through the North Channel and the Irish Sea. The survey agreement with Eire means that Soviet ships will again be able to monitor British submarine arrivals and departures. In the constant game of wits, the Royal Navy is now sending a pair of nuclear attack submarines with each missile boat until it has reached the safety of the Atlantic, thus giving the Russian vessels three targets to track and making it more difficult for them to establish which is which. However, the Soviet research vessels will inevitably be able to gather other useful information about NATO's seabed SOSUS underwater detection network mentioned earlier, and will be in an ideal situation to land covert Spetsnaz teams if desired.

Moreover, the sea is not the only means of access Spetsnaz has to Western Europe.

Notes Chapter Five

[1] By comparison, Soviet Embassy officials are restricted to a thirty mile radius of the Embassy without obtaining prior clearance.

[2] Known to Western naval intelligence as AGIs – 'Auxiliary Vessels, Miscellaneous, Intelligence'.

[3] Victor Gollancz, 1983. Quotation by kind permission of the author, via NTS, the Alliance of Russian Solidarists, an anti-Communist organization in Britain which, among other things, prepares a weekly situation report on Soviet affairs for *The Times*.

[4] And elsewhere, of course.

[5] Medium capacity fishing trawlers.

[6] This Czech-made weapon is not standard Warsaw Pact issue outside Czechoslovakia, although it is widely used by guerrilla forces around the world. It *is*, however, used by Spetsnaz and other special forces because its small size and light weight make it easy to conceal. Weighing only 2 kg loaded with a ten-round magazine, it is only 269 mm long when the wire stock is folded. It can also be fitted with a silencer.

[7] These are towed on cables behind the ship to distance them as far as possible from ambient noise which can distort the returns from fixed arrays.

Chapter Six
The TIR connection

After the third packet of photographs taken by our friend Kevin Skinner in Germany failed to arrive, we became certain that our mail was being intercepted. Kevin, a freelance photographer, had been briefed to keep his eyes open for Eastern Bloc trucks entering the West and to keep notes, identify them and look for any signs of their drivers and co-drivers displaying untoward interest in NATO bases or troop movements. This arrangement dated from March 1988.

Why were we interested?

For several years it has been known that Warsaw Pact countries have been using the TIR, or *Transport Internationale Routier*, agreement as a shield for their espionage activities in Western Europe. The TIR agreement, signed in 1949, allows lorries with bonded cargo to drive across the borders of signatory countries without being subjected to customs checks. This means that their trailers could contain *anything*, from electronic surveillance equipment to commando squads to nuclear weapons, and no-one would be any the wiser. The agreement was arrived at in order to facilitate trade and do away with unnecessary red tape during the rebuilding period following the Second World War, and has remained in force ever since.

The first public indication that the Warsaw Pact countries were using their trucks for espionage came in 1980 when defector Ilya Dschirkvelov was widely reported in the press as saying that 'All Soviet truck drivers and co-drivers on West German roads are by profession tank commanders and officers of the Red Army. They are gathering information on every road, street and bridge.' More recently, press attention has been drawn to the distinct possibility that, in addition to tank commanders, many Eastern Bloc drivers and/or co-drivers are members of Spetsnaz and other Warsaw Pact commando units, reconnoitring their objectives and the general lay of the land.

On 4 January 1987 *The Sunday Express* quoted a 'British intelligence officer based in West Germany'.

'It is a disturbing escalation in the espionage war,' he told reporter John Beattie. 'Time and again we spot Eastern Bloc lorries following tortuous routes that don't make a scrap of commercial sense, but which always seem to pass sensitive military bases. How do you stop it? The TIR agreement guarantees unimpeded passage, and by no means are all the vehicles crammed with monitoring equipment. Most, in fact, carry perfectly legitimate cargo. Yet, when big NATO exercises are held there is always a big upsurge of Warsaw Pact lorries on the autobahns of West Germany and Holland.'

As we have seen in Chapter Two, the East German NVA Handbook gives implicit directions on infiltrating military convoys. During exercises, spies in trucks will be able to measure the speed and direction of convoys, the numbers of vehicles involved, see their marshalling areas, log refuelling times and intervals and gather a great deal of other useful information about NATO forces in front line Germany. When no exercise is being held, they can measure exact distances and widths of European roads, the locations of garages, the load-carrying ability of bridges, etc. One of the reasons many lorries seem to stray off the most obvious and direct routes to their destinations will be so that they can assess the narrower country roads, pinpointing places where tanks or trailer vehicles – such as tactical nuclear missile carriers – would have difficulty traversing, and noting low bridges which a military convoy might find impassable. To this end, an increasing number of Eastern Bloc private cars are being noted on West German roads. As discussed later, this is difficult to explain in an innocent manner.

But press reports are one thing, and may or may not be accurate, of course. We wanted to see whether we could discover any evidence of our own, and for this we needed someone on the ground. Kevin Skinner was an ideal choice, for over the previous two years living in West Germany he had already accumulated an impressive folio of photographs of the border and its defences on both sides. The first box of photographs he sent us showed SovBloc trucks crossing the border, and by coincidence a few days later Kevin 'phoned us to say that the US Forces radio had just broadcast a report on a man called Koch who had defected to the West 'and was considered to be of great importance because he was in charge of the East German spy truck operations'. Barely a week later Elke Falk was arrested followed by six men, as recounted in Chapter Three, but no further public mention was made of Herr Koch. We assume that he is being debriefed and the whole matter is under security wraps. This period also marked the beginning of our own problems.

On 7 April 1988 Kevin was driving past 'Rivers Barracks', a US Army artillery depot in Giessen, just as a convoy of vehicles was moving out. He drove on so as to find a vantage point where he could park and photograph the convoy, something he had often done without any repercussions. As the convoy passed, he saw that an East German truck had infiltrated itself amongst the US vehicles. He followed the convoy for two or three kilometres until US military and West German police halted the middle section and directed the East German truck to pull over. Kevin stopped and tried to remain inconspicuous. The police checked the driver's papers but made no effort to check the truck's contents, it being protected by TIR plates. After some 25 minutes they let the truck go. When Kevin tried to take some more photographs, he was stopped by the police who also asked to see his own papers.

Kevin telephoned details of the incident and promised that the two photographs he had managed to take would be posted by recorded delivery in a sealed box. They never arrived. A few weeks later they arrived back at Kevin's home, marked 'return to sender'. The box and its contents were thoroughly waterlogged and the transparencies damaged. The post office was unable to give Kevin any explanation.

On 10 May Kevin was parked in a layby on the B3 road south of Kassel, a stopping place much favoured by German and American military vehicles because of a hot dog van which is usually parked there. Kevin was photographing some US Army vehicles when an East German truck pulled up on the other side of the road. Immediately an American Jeep detached itself and pulled up immediately in front of the truck

Russian 'spy trawlers' are festooned with aerials from stem to stern.

A Soviet 'trawler' shadows HMS *Intrepid*.

The Soviet 'research vessel' *Chumikan*. Similar vessels may soon be patrolling the Irish Sea.

The package of photographs which had been opened and the transparencies sliced from their frames.

A typical East German TIR truck. The youngish-looking co-driver appeared furious at Kevin Skinner for taking this photo.

A convoy of American M1 Abrams tanks followed closely by an East German truck.

Here another Deutrans truck pursues US tanks.

An East German truck passes a column of Abrams tanks going in the opposite direction.

Rotterdam is full of Ro-Tir trucks which are often parked for days on end without being unloaded.

Customs-sealed containers could be used to transport weapons and equipment from East to West. They could also house people.

Container barges – this one is Polish – are another common sight in Rotterdam. Installations such as the Shell refinery in the background would be obvious targets for sabotage teams.

The Soviet cruise liner *Estonia* moored opposite the Dutch Marines headquarters. This vessel also visits Scotland and the Scottish islands.

The Soviet freighter *Skuaptor Tomskia* in Rotterdam. The large crane in the stern seems more powerful than the size of the hold warrants.

The submarine construction yard at Rotterdam.

Military equipment parked on the quayside.

It is easy for GRU operatives to photograph Western warships. We obtained this shot of HMS *Argonaut* undergoing refit in Plymouth with no difficulty.

while a Ford pick-up parked right behind it, making it impossible to move. The driver of the front Jeep got out and opened his bonnet, but to Kevin it was obvious that the 'breakdown' was just a pretext.

Kevin spoke to the officer in charge of the American troops in the layby, a female Captain. She refused to say anything 'for the record' but confirmed unofficially that it was standard practice to prevent Eastern Bloc vehicles of any sort getting close to US military convoys. However, she maintained the fiction that the foremost Jeep had stopped because of a breakdown. Under normal circumstances in a case like this, if the breakdown had been genuine, you would have expected the truck driver and co-driver to ask if there was anything they could do to help, because a bona fide commercial vehicle would not want its schedule to be interrupted. Instead, the two men remained in their cab and made no attempt to communicate with the Americans. At this point US MPs and West German police arrived and confiscated the film in Kevin's camera before demanding that he leave the scene. Fortunately he had also taken a couple of frames with a second camera which are reproduced in the plate section. Part of the reason for the American concern could be the fact that the men in the background are identifiably members of a US Special Forces detachment.

Again Kevin posted his photographs to us, followed a few days later by a written report on the two incidents and details of a ban-the-bomb rally which had been attended by West German Army conscripts. Neither package arrived.

We discussed the problem with Kevin when he next visited England, and agreed that in future he would use a different post office to send his material to an accommodation address in London, where we could pick it up.

Back in Germany a few days later, Kevin received a strange telephone call from a man claiming to represent a photo library. He wanted to buy Kevin's photographs. Not a selection, the lot. He would, he said, pay well. Kevin said he would think it over. The man called again next day and repeated his request. This time Kevin asked him what specific subject areas interested him, and also said that he was reluctant to assign the copyright. The man said he was interested in anything military or connected with the border, but really wanted to buy everything. Kevin again said he would consider the proposition, and asked for a telephone number.

It is normally impossible for a member of the general public to obtain an address from a telephone number, but for obvious reasons police computers can do this. Journalists have many contacts and Kevin asked a friend of his whether he could trace the address. His friend said he wanted nothing to do with it, that Kevin should not 'get on the wrong side of the people on the "other side" ', and that his best advice was to comply with the request and sell his photographs.

When Kevin failed to telephone the 'picture library' the anonymous man called him again. This time his questions were more specific. Did Kevin have any photos which could cause embarrassment to the West German government? No! Did he have anything that could embarrass the American or British governments? No!! Did he have any photos of transport? Bingo! Again Kevin said 'no', explaining that he had had some but had disposed of them. The man on the other end of the line appeared quite upset at this and told Kevin that if any were ever published 'it will be better if you are not still in Germany'.

On Friday, 8 July, Kevin left home with another packet of photographs for us, to be mailed to the accommodation address, with a set of duplicates which would go to Mike Welham's home in Norfolk. His car was followed by a white Lada carrying East German plates and occupied by two men in their thirties. He did not post the packages that day but telephoned on the 12th to say that he was pretty certain he had not been tailed and had successfully posted the two packets. But, he said, the white Lada had been parked all day outside his local post office, with the same two men in it.

If it had been the *West* German authorities intercepting Kevin's mail, one would have expected them to send a police officer to warn him against photographing these type of subjects. The law would allow them to confiscate all Kevin's files and camera equipment. The fact that the mail was being interfered with, and the presence of the Lada, suggests that East German intelligence has infiltrated the West German post office.

A couple of days later Kevin 'phoned to say that the second batch of transparencies he had posted to us in May had been returned to him. The packet had been opened with a razor blade and two of the four transparencies were missing. Since the third batch had still not arrived, either at the accommodation address or Mike's home, he decided that he and his wife Jackie should go to Germany themselves and physically bring the photographs back to England. While there, they could also assess the situation for themselves.

* * *

A major Warsaw Pact exercise was scheduled to start on Sunday, 24 July, and this seemed an ideal time to make the trip, for NATO forces would be more on the alert than usual and this could be expected to provoke more intense activity by Eastern Bloc spy trucks. Mike and Jackie stayed at Marburg, which is surrounded by American and West German military units and conveniently close to the border. A relevant point to make here is that certain roads and stretches of autobahn in West Germany are closed to heavy traffic at weekends to create greater freedom for private motorists visiting friends and relatives or going on holiday. Arriving on a Friday, therefore, and setting out with Kevin for the border on Saturday morning, Mike and Jackie expected to see fewer trucks of any type than usual.

Approaching the border, what did they see but a convoy of four Hungarian trucks. Kevin was astonished, saying that in two years he had never encountered such a phenomenon. In the next hour and a half they identified no fewer than 21 Hungarian, East German and Polish trucks compared with a mere *five* of Western nationalities.

Coming to a major East-West border crossing point with a large car park, they saw several Eastern Bloc trucks parked, most of them belonging to the East German state trucking company Deutrans. There was nothing to stop photographs being taken, although Kevin said that on occasion the driver of an Eastern vehicle would complain to the West German police, who would ask you to move on. There was a steady flow of vehicles coming over from the East, a comparative trickle of Western trucks moving in the opposite direction.

Throughout the day Mike, Jackie and Kevin saw many more Eastern trucks, and also a surprising number of East German, Czech and Polish cars, many of them close to military installations. On Sunday there were fewer trucks but even more cars, Ladas and Skodas for the most part. Kevin said this was most unusual. The majority of SovBloc visitors to West Germany are elderly East Germans who are freely allowed to visit relations in the West. If they decide to stay, they are no loss to the East, and in fact the East German government makes a profit through no longer having to house, feed and clothe them. Moreover, it is generally only older people in the East who can afford cars at all, for they are very expensive (even though a Lada is about the cheapest car you can buy in the West) and there are long waiting lists. Younger people who can obtain a car are therefore those who, through merit, Party status or work for the government, can afford to jump the queue. Or, of course, those engaged in official work who have an official car allocated to them.

While East Germans can visit West Germany fairly freely, the same is not true of Poles, Czechs, Hungarians or Romanians, so on this particular Sunday it was even more unusual to see a fair sprinkling of cars bearing the number plates of these countries. Their occupants were single, couples or apparent family groups, but what was so interesting to them along all the border roads? Surely tourists would want to venture further afield? And how did people other than East Germans gain access to Western currency, with the rigid controls on it in the SovBloc? Moreover, why did the East German border guards allow them through so freely, when other people are dying in escape attempts to reach the West?

On Monday Mike, Jackie and Kevin resumed their prowling around, and soon lost track of the number of Eastern Bloc trucks they passed. One incident puzzled them. Approaching a border crossing point on a dual carriageway, they came up behind a beige Lada carrying Polish plates which was chugging along at a bare 30 mph. They suspected an elderly couple out for a drive but decided to follow the Lada for a while out of interest. The Lada increased speed a couple of times but then resumed its plodding pace. Coming up to an intersection, it looked as though the Lada was going to continue straight ahead, but at the last moment it swung off without indicating. On the new road, the Lada slowed right down to about 20 mph and hugged the verge, inviting the following car to overtake. Since Kevin knew there were no turn-offs for a while, they did overtake and were astonished to see, looking back, that far from being driven by an elderly couple, it was a couple in their apparent twenties.

The trio pulled into a layby to allow the Lada to get in front again, then resumed pursuit. The Lada slowed down at every road junction, and at other places, constantly varying its speed in a most erratic and unusual fashion. As the two cars approached the last exit giving access to the border crossing point, it appeared that the Lada was going to go straight on. Just past the intersection, however, it stopped at the side of the road, forcing Mike, Jackie and Kevin to overtake, then reversed rapidly back and shot up the intersection towards the border.

Quite possibly there was nothing sinister about the couple's behaviour, but it seemed most odd.

Next Kevin directed the car up a track leading towards a US Army border observation post, where they encountered four of the latest American M1 Abrams tanks, massive slab-sided beasts with laminate armour, either a 105 or a 120 mm gun, computerized fire control system with laser sighting and a powerful gas turbine engine which gives a remarkable turn of speed. Kevin turned up to the border itself to see if there was any indication of activity on the other side, then retraced the route as the tanks started moving out, catching them up just as the last two were joining the narrow access road.

The tanks belted off down the road, forcing incoming vehicles into the roadside to give them passage. Coming to a 'T' junction, the tanks stopped until a gap appeared in the traffic then swung out, joining a road which would either take them back towards the border or give them access to an autobahn. Several Hungarian trucks passed in the opposite direction. Across another 'T' junction Kevin was able to overtake the tanks and began looking for a place to stop in order to photograph them. Finding a layby, the trio parked and got out of the car. As the tanks roared past with a clatter of tracks Kevin got busy with his camera, for they were now being closely followed by a Deutrans truck.

Back in the car, the trio caught up with the convoy after about a kilometre, but the truck had disappeared. The only conclusion we could draw is that the driver had been alarmed at being photographed and had standing orders to cover such an eventuality, so had turned off. This could only have been on to a minor country road totally unsuitable for large lorries.

Later, the trio were travelling along a dual carriageway towards Bad Hersfeld, home from home of the US 11th Armored Cavalry, when they overtook an East German truck. Passing the base down a long hill, they could look out over the valley at the tanks and other vehicles parked in the perimeter. As they ascended the hill on the other side of the valley, they realized that the truck was no longer behind them. Since there were no side roads, it must have stopped somewhere overlooking the base. Such incidents are fairly common, although the most famous of all must be that recorded in the *Reader's Digest* of December 1986.

'The East German juggernaut had been parked on the perimeter of a US Army base near Stuttgart for several days in 1984 when an accidental fire burned through its outer casing, revealing sensitive eavesdropping equipment. The device was so sophisticated that it could pick up the impulses of electric typewriters in the base.' If this seems improbable, almost science fiction in fact, the respected science writer Doug Richardson has the following to say in his book *Techniques and Equipment of Electronic Warfare*[1]. 'The internal circuitry within computer equipment operates at frequencies within the normal range used for radio communications. As a result, the computer tends to radiate electrical noise as individual elements in its internal circuitry "broadcast" the data that they are handling ... From the military viewpoint, such unwanted emissions also provide an additional method of espionage.'

Next day, Tuesday 26 July, Mike and Jackie left Kevin to head back towards Holland, eyes opened to the extent of Eastern vehicular traffic close to NATO bases in West Germany. (After stopping outside the 11th Armored base to wait for the East German truck they had overtaken, they counted 25 other Deutrans vehicles, 17 of other Warsaw Pact nationalities and one Russian refrigerated truck in the space of an hour. Some 450,000 SovBloc trucks enter Western Europe each year, according to official statistics.)

Before leaving the West German scene, though, one further incident is relevant. The photographs which Kevin had posted after escaping the Lada's surveillance in July did, eventually, turn up in England over a month later, on 16 August. The yellow cardboard box had been opened and resealed with Royal Mail sticky tape. Inside were four transparency frames. The slides themselves had been removed from within them. There was no accompanying letter, nothing from HM Customs and Excise, no explanation at all. And no way of telling whether the packet had been opened on the Continent or after arrival in the UK.

As Ian Fleming wrote: 'Once is happenstance, twice is coincidence, but three times is enemy action'.

* * *

The drive back to Holland was uneventful although on one motorway flyover close to Schipol airport Mike and Jackie saw a Deutrans truck parked in the middle of the bridge. A breakdown is, of course, the probable explanation, but the truck crew could alternatively have been surveying the bridge and its environs.

As already noted, Rotterdam is a key centre for Eastern Bloc trade and espionage activity in Western Europe. It is also one of the principal ports through which reinforcements for the British Army of the Rhine would be shipped in time of war. We have a friend, who wishes to remain anonymous, who over a period of six months has closely observed shipping and truck activity there on our behalf. Of particular note, he has seen that lorries of the Romanian state trucking company Ro-Tir are not only extremely common but tend to stay in the harbour for prolonged periods and to do their loading and unloading at weekends when everything is relatively quiet. The Ro-Tir company terminal in Holland is on the dockside opposite the harbour radar installation and practically alongside the Royal Netherlands Marines Korps HQ. It is also only some 400 m from the giant Euromast telecommunications tower and 50 m from the entrance to the Maas Tunnel, the principal route for vehicles and pedestrians under the harbour.

On 3 July 1988, for example, there were six vessels docked alongside, flying British, Dutch, Norwegian and West German flags. On the dockside were three Western TIR container trailers, minus their tractor units which had departed for other work. However, there were *twelve* Ro-Tir trucks and trailers present, whose crews remained in their cabs for the most part although they would occasionally converse with each other. Despite the presence of two cafes at either end of the dock, the Ro-Tir crews remained with their vehicles (which, like most long-distance lorries, have their own cooking and sleeping facilities). Two days later, while the Western trailers and all but the Norwegian ship had gone, nine of the twelve Ro-Tir trucks were still there. Commercially, this is a complete waste of time, money and manpower and would not be tolerated by a Western company unless there was an ulterior motive.

Our friend also noted that, whilst most of the Ro-Tir drivers and co-drivers were middle aged and rather overweight, on this particular occasion he saw one who seemed totally out of place. He was about thirty and in good physical condition, but was seen carrying an attaché case which at other times he kept carefully locked in his cab.

Romanian trucks are not the only ones to use Rotterdam. East German Deutrans and VK vehicles are common, as are those of the Czech CSAD company, Hungarocamion from Budapest, Pekaes from Warsaw and Sovtrans from Russia, the latter being the least common, however. Perhaps it is coincidence, but Polish Ocean Lines have a railway terminal for Polish and East German rolling stock on the wharf opposite Ro-Tir, adjacent to the other end of the Maas Tunnel and the radar station.

The Soviet ro-ro vessel *Inzhener Nechiporenko* was also in Rotterdam at this time, undergoing repair. Why, one wonders, should the Soviet Union spend hard currency having such work done in a Western port when a Russian, Polish or East German yard could do it so much more cheaply? Perhaps the fact that Dutch 'Walrus' Class submarines were being built in the dockyard, where they could be photographed in detail from the Russian vessel, might help explain it. The brand-new 'Walrus' Class boats are being built to replace the older 'Zwaardvis' Class and will have superior diving performance as well as GEC Avionics towed array sonar and a new Hollandse signal processing system, both of which would be of immense interest to the GRU.

Earlier in the year, in May, a Polish naval training vessel called at Rotterdam. Our friend observed that while all the officers, crewmen and cadets wore uniform, there were five men aboard who wore casual civilian clothing and never ventured ashore. Three were apparently in their twenties and two in their forties. All had short haircuts, but not naval short back and sides. When crew members left the ship, past the three armed guards permanently stationed at the gangway, they invariably did so in uniform. So who were the five 'civilians'?

Other regular visitors to the port include Soviet cruise liners which frequently moor at the Holland-Amerika jetty directly opposite the Marine Korps headquarters and in an ideal situation from which to take photographs.

The Dutch authorities have remained totally silent on the subject of possible GRU/Spetsnaz activities in Holland, neither letters nor telephone calls having produced any response. Unofficially, however, we have learned that Dutch security forces have followed Eastern Bloc trucks, and that on one occasion a Romanian lorry took *five days* to get from the West German border to Rotterdam, normally a distance of scarcely a hundred miles. Its tortuous route took it past every defence establishment between the border and the coast. On another occasion, we have been told, Eastern Bloc lorry drivers have been spotted by the Dutch security police measuring the depth of a river, presumably to ascertain where tanks could ford it in the event of the bridges being demolished. The only evidence that the Dutch authorities are tightening up on the situation at all is that they have introduced a recent ruling that for every SovBloc TIR truck allowed into Holland, a Dutch truck has to enter the Eastern zone. Quite what this achieves remains a mystery!

* * *

We spoke to one retired Dutch long-distance truck driver who, once he understood the line of questioning, asked to remain anonymous. As we had already seen, people who have any first-hand knowledge of possible Spetsnaz activities are generally scared to talk about it. This particular driver told us that he used to work for a company which had a contract with the Dutch Ministry of Defence. It was a good, steady job with no tight schedules which took him in and out of defence establishments, usually air bases, where he would load up with prepacked containers. He normally drove alone, without a co-driver, whereas Eastern Bloc lorries almost invariably have two men aboard. In his personal experience, they *always* had two.

His routeing frequently took him into West Germany and then on down into Italy, another partner in NATO. On one particular occasion, he told us, he had to deliver some engines to Italy for overhaul, with a stop *en route* in Germany. As he pulled away from the air base after loading, he began looking for his 'tail', for he had already observed on previous trips that before he had gone very far a Warsaw Pact truck would start following him. The nationality was usually East German but sometimes Bulgarian, particularly on journeys into France where the Bulgarian Mat company has a virtual monopoly on TIR haulage through undercutting other firms by as much as fifty per cent.

The truck following was not always the same. Sometimes one would turn off and a different one pick up the trail, but there was always one in evidence. Whenever he stopped, the

Dutchman told us, to refuel or simply to relieve himself, his 'tail' stopped too. It happened so often that it had ceased to concern him, and in fact had become something of a joke between himself and other drivers who had noticed the same thing.

In common with truck drivers around the world, he would often stop at transport cafes for a meal, a drink, and a gossip with friends and acquaintances. Once in a while the Eastern Bloc drivers would sit with them, especially if the place was crowded. The co-drivers always remained with their vehicles. On this occasion the driver of the following truck was East German, and since the Dutchman spoke German they conversed of general things. Then he asked the driver about his 'mate'. The German shrugged, said 'Russki' and left the answer at that. On a couple of other occasions 'our' driver had noted that the co-drivers would actually leave their vehicle for the express purpose of ordering the drivers away from where they were sitting with Western drivers, clearly showing who was in charge.

When he reached his destination, the driver said, the following truck would disappear, but it would not be many minutes after he left that it, or a similar vehicle, would be back on his tail. Confirming absolutely conclusively that the tailing is deliberate, our driver said that sometimes an Eastern Bloc truck would follow him from Holland, through Germany, down into Italy and then all the way back to Holland, without ever unloading or loading anything itself.

The driver told us of another significant incident. Pulling into a garage to refuel one day, he noticed an East German tractor unit just departing. He mentioned it casually to the pump attendant, who shrugged and said it had been backwards and forwards for three days with minor faults caused, not by mechanical failure, but by bad driving. As he continued on his way, our driver passed the East German truck as it was recoupling with its trailer, parked in a layby. Nothing strange in that – but the trailer had been parked for three days outside an American air base ...

* * *

The Norwegian authorities, who were the first to wake up to spying activities by Warsaw Pact trucks, have been more forthcoming than the Dutch. We spoke to their Military Attaché in London and asked whether Norway had had any problems similar to those in Sweden with divers and mini-subs. No, we were told, although regular Soviet submarines had to be chased away on occasion. As far as trucks are concerned, however, in 1983 the commander of Norway's Northern Region, General Ulf Berg, called for a clampdown. This followed one particular incident when a Sovtrans truck which had driven the 868 miles from Leningrad to Tromsø spent a week loitering in the port – a vital NATO installation. The truck's cargo was dried herrings, which you could say was the same as taking coals to Newcastle ... Since then the Norwegian authorities have exploited Article 20 of the TIR Convention, which states that 'For journeys in the territory of their own country, the customs authorities may fix a time limit and require the road vehicle ... to follow a prescribed route'. Eastern Bloc countries have *always* imposed this restriction on Western trucks entering their own territory.

Despite these regulations, it is inevitable that Spetsnaz personnel are still able to observe and measure things which will be valuable intelligence to an invasion force[2].

Sweden is also as much aware of the truck problem as it is of the coastal incursions. Mr Thomas Gür, Press Officer at the Swedish Department of Defence, told us in a letter that:

'As most of the material on the suspected movements of the aforementioned trucks are classified, I have had some difficulties in obtaining nonclassified documents.

'Please find enclosed a declassified study from 1986 on the movements of the trucks and two answers from 1987 and 1988 given by this authority on the same issue.'

The documents he supplied showed that Sweden established regulations as long ago as 1974 requiring foreign truck drivers entering the country to notify the authorities of their destination and route, for 'although operating under the international agreement, the number of vehicles had dramatically increased and could be considered out of control'. The Swedish government would continue to honour the TIR agreement but required foreign transport companies to furnish details which would enable the authorities to control their vehicles in transit. 'Sweden has a difficult problem', the documents state, 'for it has borders and links with countries of both the East and West and so trucks come from the Soviet

Union, Poland and East Germany and pass on to countries such as West Germany, Denmark and Norway. That in itself is one problem but it is the route that the trucks take that is the bigger one.'

The last reference was to the recognized fact that many trucks were taking circuitous routes which took them past defence establishments. The Swedish authorities had also noted that the co-drivers of Eastern trucks invariably had cameras, either still or in some cases video, and this takes us back to Kevin Skinner in Germany.

On Thursday, 11 August 1988, Kevin was driving into Giessen past the US Army artillery depot – or rather through it, because it stretches either side of the road – when he spotted a parked car. Beside it were a man and a woman with a video camera. The car's number plates were Hungarian. Apart from the road itself, there was nothing to film except the base, so the couple's interest had to be military. Kevin drove up to the guardhouse and reported the couple, but was told there was nothing the authorities could do. Unlike Britain, which closely restricts photography from roadsides adjacent to airfields, etc, West Germany has no such law.

One obvious question is whether East Bloc TIR trucks are also operative in the UK. The answer is that they do visit, most being Czech, but have not been observed doing anything suspicious. The reasons are twofold. In case of war there would be no Warsaw Pact armoured Blitzkrieg up British motorways. Moreover, as we have established, most GRU/Spetsnaz infiltration of the UK is by sea.

* * *

While the East Germans, Czechs and other Warsaw Pact nations tend to use trucks for their long-distance haulage, the Soviet Union prefers the railways. There is no evidence that Russian flatbed containers are ever used for espionage purposes, but the West obviously uses this method, as the following story illustrates. And if the West, it is only logical to assume that the East does as well.

'Russians seize "spy laboratory" on goods train' screamed *The Times* on 11 June 1987. A Reuter report from Moscow said that a freight container being shipped from Yokohama in Japan via the Russian port of Nakhodka and the Trans-Siberian Railway to Hamburg in West Germany had been stopped in Moscow. The Soviet authorities had been alerted by 'blue light flashing through a ventilation duct and … a muffled humming noise coming from the container'. Quoting the Russian paper *Izvestia*, the report said, 'A whole espionage laboratory was hidden behind a box of clay pots'. Computers, geiger counters and cameras were said to be amongst the Soviets' haul, and immediate protests lodged with the Japanese and West German governments. Much of the equipment was said to be of American manufacture.

If they can travel by truck and ship and car, they could certainly travel by train, or bus, or 'plane, these men of Spetsnaz. And a convenient disguise is as a member of a sports team.

Notes Chapter Six

[1] Salamander Books, 1985.

[2] Of interest here, especially when seen in the context of Soviet infiltration of both peace groups and underground guerrilla organizations discussed in Chapter 9, is the fact that *The Guardian* reported on 29 June 1988 that explosives, grenades and ammunition had been stolen from Norwegian army depots on two separate occasions, the first involving the theft of 2,000 rounds of smallarms ammunition and twenty hand grenades and the second a fortnight later 65 lb of explosives and 3,000 rounds of ammunition. The authorities attributed the thefts to 'urban terrorists' but it is possible that the group or groups involved could be among those who might help Spetsnaz teams in time of war. If this *were* the case, such raids could possibly be a form of 'feasibility study' to see how easy or difficult it would be to acquire munitions for back-up operations. As in other instances, the apparent lack of real official interest poses several questions. It is inconceivable that the authorities could simply not care when such weaponry is stolen, so it is logical to assume that the mask of official indifference is a cover to conceal the real counter-terrorist activities of the security forces which we can only assume are happening.

Chapter Seven
Sportsnaz?

The Red Army defector who writes under the pseudonym Viktor Suvorov makes a great deal of the supposed fact that virtually every member of Soviet sports teams competing in the West, male and female, is a member of Spetsnaz. As we have seen earlier, he even names one athlete whom our own research proves to be a figment of the imagination, so the whole subject deserves closer examination.

Certainly a large number of Soviet athletes are members of the armed forces, nor does the Russian government seek to hide the fact. Of 520 Soviet athletes taking part in the Seoul Olympics, many will undoubtedly have been members of the Army, Navy and Air Force[1], but no figures were available at the time of writing. Since every man in the Warsaw Pact countries has to undertake between eighteen months' and three years' military service from the age of eighteen, this is fully understandable. The ages of eighteen to twenty are crucial in any athlete's development. He or she is reaching the peak of physical maturity, dexterity, stamina and co-ordination. These are obviously requirements for members of Spetsnaz as well, but to extrapolate from this that all Soviet sportsmen and women are therefore members of Spetsnaz is fanciful.

From previous years, a large number of Soviet athletes are acknowledged members of the armed forces. Serik Nurkazov, gold, silver and bronze Olympic medal winner for boxing, is an Army PT instructor. Alexander Jagubkin, Soviet Absolute Champion in 1980, was in the armed forces. So were Vladimir Parfenovich, the yachtsman Boris Budnikov, Alexander Meletryev (a smallarms instructor), the weightlifter Anatoli Pisarenko, the judo champion Shota Khabarelli, the wrestlers

Sergei and Anatoli Beloglasov and the gymnast Bogdan Makuts[2], among hundreds of others. But members of Spetsnaz?

It *is* generally accepted that Moscow Dynamo football team is composed entirely of KGB and MVD personnel and is run by the MVD. Jim Riordan lived for five years in Moscow playing football and other sports and he makes this point plain in his book *Sport in Soviet Society*[3]. Similarly, the ZSKA male gymnastics team is composed entirely of serving Army personnel. Riordan talks about DOSAAF (see also Chapter Two) which was first formed in 1927 and whose aims, reiterated in 1971, are 'Widely to propagandize among the public, especially young people, military knowledge and the heroic traditions of the Soviet people, to improve the quality of training of young people for service in the Armed Forces, and further to promote military technical sports'. The latter obviously includes such activities as shooting, swimming, riding, climbing, skiing, cross-country running, gliding and parachuting, for example, all necessary Spetsnaz skills. And, as we have seen, membership of DOSAAF is one of the attributes which the Red Army and GRU take into account when selecting conscripts for entry into the elite Spetsnaz Brigades. The GTO, or 'Ready for Labour and Defence' organization which is responsible for most athletics training in the Soviet Union, gives instruction in the use of gas masks and grenade throwing, canoeing, judo and wrestling as well, and is part of the USSR's civil defence structure. But again, to try and make from this a case for all Soviet athletes being members of Spetsnaz is absurd.

We have already examined the Spetsnaz role, but how would membership of international sports teams aid their objectives? Certainly Soviet athletes competing abroad will have the opportunity to meet Western athletes, but packed training schedules would seem to leave little time for sufficient socializing to build up close relationships, and if recruitment to the Soviet cause was a motive, it would be hard to accomplish. Moreover, the Spetsnaz role is a covert one, so even if a given sportsman *is* a member, he would be hardly likely to reveal the fact to a Westerner.

Lack of time also seems to preclude reconnaissance in the sense of getting the feel of a Western city which might be a Spetsnaz target in time of war, or for meeting with sleeper agents in place who would help Spetsnaz teams. Naturally, members of Spetsnaz in athletic teams will keep their eyes and ears open, for we have already seen the KGB's and GRU's 'magpie' attitude towards intelligence gathering. *Everything* is seen as a potentially useful piece of information, no matter how seemingly trivial.

Successful athletes, the goal scorers and medal winners, are public figures, their backgrounds and love lives as well as their sporting accomplishments being the constant subject of media attention. In the Soviet Union, sporting achievement is rewarded with a larger apartment, a car, the opportunity to travel. But a member of a Spetsnaz team could not afford to operate in the limelight like this. His is a secret world kept closely hidden from his dearest friends and relatives.

In 1984 the Soviet parachuting team, five men and two women, won 22 out of the 26 gold medals being competed for in the World Parachuting Championship. There was speculation at the time that they might be members of Spetsnaz spying out suitable spots for covert landings. Since, in order to win so spectacularly, every ounce of each competitor's concentration must have been on the task in hand, this seems most unlikely. Moreover, suitable landing places could be better and more easily reconnoitred from the ground. On another occasion, 28 members of DOSAAF schools parachuted on to the North Pole. This was obviously just a stunt, so should not be read as evidence that they were Spetsnaz specialists trained in arctic warfare!

If there *are* members of Spetsnaz in Soviet sports teams, as seems probable but unprovable, they are most likely of all to feature in the aquatic events. Mike Welham describes selection for the Spetsnaz naval brigades in detail in his book on combat frogmen[4].

'Selection of suitable candidates for the Spetsnaz underwater units begins long before their induction into the Soviet armed forces. Those with the ability and flair are found in the DOSAAF schools. Those who undertake the sub-aqua sportsman route are divided into four groups, the first being for elementary training which includes children in the age range six to nine years … Training at this early stage is important and the instructors are very attentive in seeking out those children who could fulfil both the hopes of instructors and the military authorities …

'At thirteen to fifteen years of age, the adolescents

transfer to the elite group. Their athletic development is reaching its peak and their underwater swimming ability is improving, both in technical knowledge and endurance ... [When] physical capabilities and scuba skills are perfected, the student is prepared to become "Master of Sport of the USSR, International Class".

'The DOSAAF Naval School in Odessa is one of the centres where specialized underwater training is undertaken[5] ... The Soviet system places great store on the past struggles and primarily the enormous losses suffered by the country in the Second World War, and part of the military/political input covers the past and students constantly meet veterans of the war.

'The school's programme covers "theoretical knowledge", swimming both in pools and at sea, under as well as on the surface. Boat work and specialist underwater training using simulators is undertaken, and one can assume that when the word "simulators" is used it could cover deep diving equipment, decompression chambers and submarine lock-out training[6]. The role of a diver is far-reaching ... Inspection of ships' hulls and engineering skills are well covered, and many of the older members undertaking diver training will already have an engineering skill. In the more advanced training programmes, underwater navigation and photography are among the subjects covered.

'The school encourages all trainees to participate in sport and apart from diving and sub-aqua work, orienteering, swimming with flippers and underwater endurance swims of lengths of 200, 400, 800 and 1,500 metres are undertaken. The water skills and training are combined with shooting and many other conventional sports, sea rowing and power boat racing being especially popular ...

'The students are aware [that the instructors are seeking out] special members of their groups. Part of the overall concept of seeking those with aptitude and a dedicated intelligence is to divide the trainees into groups and generate a competitive spirit.'

The Soviet Underwater Swimming Federation, founded in 1959, now boasts a membership in excess of 100,000 and has been a member of the World Confederation of Underwater Sports since 1965. Soviet athletes currently hold all world records for underwater speed events. In the 1982 World

Championships they won all 33 gold medals available, and in the 1985 event established 21 new world records. This is the quality which members of Spetsnaz are expected to display in all their forms of activity.

The question of Spetsnaz involvement in international sport must, therefore, remain inconclusive. That such involvement exists is almost certainly true, but Suvorov undeniably gives a false impression of its sinister implications. The evidence for rather more genuinely sinister activity in another area is, however, accumulating rapidly.

Notes Chapter Seven

[1] Figures supplied by *The Daily Telegraph* Information Bureau.

[2] Extracted from the *Rothmans Atlas of World Sport* (Rothmans Publications) and the *Sony Tape Guide to the 1984 Olympics* (Pelham Books).

[3] Cambridge University Press.

[4] Also published by Patrick Stephens Ltd.

[5] By teenagers who will become regular naval personnel as well as Spetsnaz, of course.

[6] In other words, entering and leaving a submerged submarine through the escape chamber.

Chapter Eight
Murder most foul

'According to NATO intelligence experts, up to 20,000 Communist agents flooded into the West during the early 1980s with instructions to buy, beg, borrow or steal technology secrets. Russia was trying to catch up with Western advances in electronics without wasting time and resources. Posing as students and businessmen, the agents openly bought sophisticated children's computer games so Moscow could study how they were programmed. Bogus shops and businesses were started, ordering high-technology products which were later shipped behind the Iron Curtain. Targets which could not be bought were stolen from factories and exhibitions.'[1]

As we approach the 21st century, the Soviet Union is quietly waging its greatest war since the Patriotic War of 1941-45. The 'hot' war ceased, the 'cold' war began, but even in today's *glasnost* situation the unseen warriors of espionage are as active as ever, and many experts believe more so. Behind the massive world-wide operation are the faceless men and women in the various KGB and GRU Directorates described in Chapter Three, but it is increasingly clear that the personnel at the 'sharp end' of this undeclared but deadly war include members of Spetsnaz and the undercover forces of the other Warsaw Pact countries.

In June 1988 the Canadian government expelled eight Soviet Embassy officials. The move was made quietly so as not to 'rock the boat' in the wake of the Moscow Summit, but the story was leaked from within the Solicitor-General's department. The only reason given for the expulsions was the usual 'improper and unacceptable behaviour', which is diplomatic jargon for spying, but there was considerable speculation[2] that the Canadian government's action was related to its intended purchase of ten British 'Trafalgar' Class nuclear submarines over the next decade. The 'Trafalgar' Class boats are said to be the quietest of their type in the world, which would make them of obvious interest to the GRU because Russian submarines are generally noisier than their Western counterparts.

Confirmation came when it was later reported in *The New York Times* that the Soviets had tried to infiltrate Paramax Electronics in Montreal. Paramax is a subsidiary of the Unisys Corporation in America, formed by a merger between Sperry and Burroughs, and among other interests has developed sophisticated control systems for the nuclear power plants in the 'Trafalgar' Class boats. The expulsions, the paper said, followed the defection of Yuri Smurov from the International Civil Aviation Organization in Montreal.

The Canadian Minister for External Affairs, Mr Joe Clark, told Parliament of a widespread espionage operation whose purpose had been 'to secure clandestine access to classified information and sensitive technology with commercial and military applications'.

'The government acted after thorough investigations,' he continued, 'which led us to the inescapable conclusion that the Soviet officials concerned had engaged in unacceptable activities which were a threat to the security of the country.'

Earlier in the year, in January, French security took seven businessmen into custody on charges of supplying forbidden hi-tech equipment to the Eastern Bloc. It was claimed[3] that they had set up a 'front' company in Luxembourg through which they were trans-shipping American computers, and that their apprehension resulted from a Pentagon request. And *Computer News*, which until it ceased publication in September 1988 was in the forefront of investigative journalism into hi-tech leaks, reported that Soviet computer scientist Andrei Petr Ershov had criticized Western controls on exports during a symposium in Copenhagen. The magazine quoted him as saying, 'The US embargo on computer sales to Eastern Bloc countries is both foolish and inefficient ... It is impossible to start up truly efficient research co-operation internationally when we are not even able to agree upon common hardware. This sapping of all research efforts is senseless.' Mr Ershov added that 'Human ideas are abstract, and potential exchange will not be stopped by an embargo purely aimed at the equipment'.

Then, in March it was revealed that the Soviet Union had tried to buy its way into a major British scientific research project[4]. The Advanced Energy Research Institute (AERI) was set up in 1987 as a privately sponsored organization by former Coal Board Chairman Sir Iain MacGregor and businessman Mr Leonard Holihan, the idea being to prevent good ideas being lost to British industry through lack of research funding or facilities. Mr Holihan was approached by Dr Valery N. Terekhin, Second Secretary for Science and Technology[5] at the Soviet Embassy in London, who offered backing in return for access to the Institute's files, some of which are defence related. He also wanted the Institute's help in compiling a directory of British scientists 'involved in major technological breakthroughs'. Not surprisingly, Mr Holihan politely but firmly declined to accept Dr Terekhin's offer.

What is perhaps most significant about the approach, though, is the Soviets' interest in which British scientists are studying what. There are two motives for this. One is to try to find a lever – money, blackmail or whatever – to persuade such people to co-operate with the Soviet Union and pass over classified information on their research. This has happened so often over the years as dozens of spy scandals have revealed that it is no mere speculation. The other possibility is to hinder Western research by eliminating scientists who refuse to co-operate. This is by far the most blatant way in which Spetsnaz operatives and members of the KGB's Department 8, Directorate S, appear to be showing their hand today. Over the last few years, more than thirty British scientists working in defence-related hi-tech industries have died or disappeared under mysterious circumstances which cannot all be explained in any normal fashion.

* * *

The first expression of public concern came in March 1987 when Mr John Cartwright MP wrote to Lord Trefgarne, Minister of State for Defence Procurement.

> 'I am growing increasingly concerned', he said, 'about the possibility of links between the deaths of three scientists and the disappearance of a fourth, all of whom were involved in military research.

'The four cases with which I am concerned are: Vimal Dajibhai, who was found dead beneath Clifton suspension bridge, Bristol, in August last year and about whose death the Coroner recorded an open verdict; Ashad Sharif, who was found dead outside Bristol in October 1986 and about whose death the Coroner recorded a suicide verdict; Avtar Singh-Gida, who disappeared in Derbyshire in January; and David Sands, who was found dead yesterday [30 March 1987] after apparently committing suicide by driving a petrol filled car into an unused building.

'Two main factors link these four cases. Each of the individuals was a computer scientist involved in defence research. And in each case there was no obvious motive to lead any of these men to commit suicide or to disappear.

'I do not wish to be accused of inventing plots more suited to a television thriller than real life, but I think the circumstances of these four cases and the possible connections between them stretch the possibility of mere coincidence too far.

'The reason I am writing to you is that all four scientists were working on research that has potentially important defence implications. The three who have died all worked for Marconi companies; and Mr Dajibhai, Mr Sharif and Mr Singh-Gida were all working on aspects of underwater vibration simulation which has extensive implications for the Strategic Defence Initiative. I understand that Mr Sands was also involved in SDI-related research, on computer controlled radar.

'All four of these men seem to have had no good reason to take their own lives, or in Mr Singh-Gida's case to disappear. They were well-balanced successful professionals who had a great deal to live for.'

Vimal Dajibhai, aged 24, was a computer expert working on naval wargames simulation for Marconi Underwater Systems at Croxley Green, near Watford, a company whose projects include the Royal Navy's latest Stingray torpedo. On the day in question, he left a note for his wife saying he was taking the car and would be home late. He never returned, and the following morning his body was found at the foot of Clifton suspension bridge, across the other side of Britain from his north London home. Neither colleagues nor friends knew of any reason why he should have wanted to go to Bristol in the first place, and even less of why he should have thrown himself off the bridge, for he had just secured a new and highly paid job in London.

Certain bizarre aspects of the situation resulted in two post mortems taking place. The body was found with its trousers half pulled down, and there was a small puncture mark on the left buttock which aroused suspicion. In the car was a bottle of red wine and two paper cups. Dajibhai was a teetotaler. His family asked that the cups be investigated to see whether saliva traces would show that Dajibhai had drunk from one, but if this was done they were not informed.

It was a similar puncture mark which led to the discovery of what had killed Georgi Markov in 1978 (see page 63). Was there someone else in the car with Dajibhai?

Two months later 26-year-old Ashad Sharif, who worked for Marconi Defence at Stamford, Lincolnshire, was also found dead in Bristol. Prior to this he had worked for Marconi Underwater Systems at Portsmouth. The only tenuous connection he had with Bristol was that he had once worked for British Aerospace. He was found in his car, a length of nylon rope tied around his neck and the other end tied to a tree. He had garrotted himself ... or had someone else tied the fatal knots and set the car in motion?

Sharif's family were advised not to attend the inquest, at which the Coroner, Mr Donald Hawkins, recorded a verdict of suicide. We contacted the Coroner ourselves, but found him most unhelpful. He refused to talk about either the Sharif or the Dajibhai case, and said nothing could be made available, especially if we were writing a book. In fact the Coroner refused to supply a transcript of the inquest proceedings to anyone, including the family. However, he has subsequently been quoted[6] as saying there could be 'a James Bond connection' between the deaths of Dajibhai and Sharif.

The member of Sharif's family who travelled to Bristol to identify the body and recover the car, an Audi automatic, noticed two strange things. There were three cigars in the car – but Sharif did not smoke and had even gone to the trouble of putting a 'no smoking' sticker in the car. Even stranger was the fact that the car's wheelbrace was on the floor alongside the accelerator pedal. Could it have been wedged there? No satisfactory answers have ever emerged and so far as the family know the police disregarded both items. Dr Desmond Kelly, a leading London psychiatrist was later quoted in *The*

Independent Magazine as saying the case was 'extraordinarily bizarre' and that in thirty years' practice he had never heard of a similar case.

In January 1987 Avtar Singh-Gida disappeared in Derbyshire. As a PhD student at Loughborough University, he was working on a Ministry of Defence financed project concerned with underwater acoustic imaging and helping to produce a report on a high-powered sonar transmitter. He and a colleague were conducting an experiment at a reservoir near Ticknall in Derbyshire. The two men went off separately for lunch, but Singh-Gida did not return. His friend raised the alarm and a police search was instituted, divers searching the bottom of the reservoir, but no body was found. Investigations showed that he had no domestic, financial or study problems, so what reason could he have for disappearing a week before finishing his doctorate?

Vimal Dajibhai had studied at Loughborough, lived in the same hall of residence as Singh-Gida, and had been acquainted with him.

Questions in parliament failed to produce any satisfactory answers. On 23 March 1987 Mr Dale Campbell-Savours (Labour MP for Workington) asked the Secretary of State for Defence, Archie Hamilton, whether he would list all research contracts his department had with universities in the UK and with Marconi, in connection with SDI[7]. Mr Hamilton said there were no such contracts with universities. 'A number of SDI research awards (known as letters of offer and acceptance) have been placed on the MoD by the US Government,' he continued. 'In turn the majority of the work in each study area has been contracted to British companies by the MoD. In this respect Marconi Ltd is under contract in the following studies: European architecture study; Battle management/command, control, communications; and the European test bed.'

The answer was obviously evasive, and it is difficult to see how a study of European architecture can be related to the Strategic Defence Initiative.

Mr Campbell-Savours then asked the Secretary of State what contracts his department had with Loughborough University for research, and into what subjects. Mr Hamilton replied, 'The MoD has fifteen research agreements with Loughborough University covering a range of defence related topics. It is up to the university itself to decide whether to make further information available.' In other words, although denying that any British university was handling research connected with SDI, Loughborough *was* undertaking defence research. It could, however, be argued that any research into underwater acoustics has relevance to SDI, so the answer was again evasive.

Two days later[8], Mr John Cartwright asked the Secretary of State for the Home Office, Mr Douglas Hurd, whether he would cause to be published the reports of the Avon and Somerset Constabularies into the deaths of Dajibhai and Sharif. Mr Hurd said, 'The publication of the police report following an investigation is a matter for the Chief Constable. It is not normal practice to publish material other than that submitted in evidence; to do so would discourage members of the public from co-operating fully with the police.' Under the strange circumstances of both deaths, and in the face of mounting public concern, it might perhaps have been more prudent to issue some form of document, even if it had to be 'doctored' to protect the innocent or hide facts related to national security. In fact, Mr Eric Deakin (then Labour MP for Walthamstow) did raise the latter question a few days later[9] when he asked the Secretary of State for Defence whether Mr Sharif, who committed suicide in Bristol on 28 October 1986, had been involved in work of a classified nature.

Mr Deakin also asked during what period Sharif worked for defence contractors on projects financed by public funds and whether his work was subject to current investigations by MoD police at Marconi in Portsmouth. Mr Hamilton said, 'Mr Sharif was employed by Marconi Defence Systems plc from 24 June 1985 until his death. His work did not entail access to information classified above "restricted". He was employed at Stanmore, not Portsmouth.' But, on 8 April, in response to a further question from Mr Deakin[10], the Secretary of State admitted that Sharif had worked at Portsmouth for three days a week during January to March 1986. So why the earlier denial that he had worked at Portsmouth?

Avtar Singh-Gida surfaced again in Paris in May and returned home to his wife. When interviewed, he said he had been confused. 'I did not plan to disappear, it was a result of pressure of work.' He refused to say why he had gone to Paris or how he had got there. Partial amnesia following a nervous breakdown? Or could he have been drugged? He was interviewed by an official from the Ministry of Defence, but what he told him has not been made public, nor will Mr Singh-Gida talk to anyone else about his disappearance.

In fact, all our attempts to talk to people connected with the deaths and disappearances we have investigated have met with stony walls of silence apart from emphatic denials, in those cases where suicide verdicts have been recorded, that the men concerned could have committed suicide.

On 30 March 1987 Mr David Sands placed two five-gallon drums of petrol in his car and drove it at an estimated 80 mph into a disused cafe alongside the A33 road at Popham, near Basingstoke. He died in the ensuing fireball and left a wife and two children.

Mr Sands was a 37-year-old project manager at Easams Ltd, a member of the GEC group with headquarters at Camberley, in Surrey. Of its 900 staff, 150 were then involved in operational assessment of defence related projects. (Marconi is also part of the GEC group.) All their work is highly sensitive and includes the computerized missile fire control system on the Sea Harrier. At the time of his death Mr Sands was himself working on the UK Air project, a new system which will link mobile ground-based radars with airborne early warning and command systems and air defence aircraft. The system is designed to reduce the vulnerability of existing fixed radar installations to both aerial attack and sabotage by Spetsnaz teams.

Three days before he died, Mr Sands had disappeared from home and his worried wife telephoned the police. The following day Special Branch officers called at his office and were actually there when his wife 'phoned to say all was well, he had returned. No explanation has ever been given for his absence, nor was the question raised at the inquest – so where had he been and, perhaps more significantly, whom had he seen?

His father-in-law says that he was not depressed, and that in fact the family had just returned from a holiday in Venice. His wife confirmed at the inquest that he was happy at work and that his only worry at the time was for his father, who was dying. The Coroner recorded an open verdict.

Three men dead and one disappearance. First link: they were all involved in defence-related projects. Second link: two of them worked for Marconi and one for a sister company. Third link: two of them knew each other. Fourth link: two of them made unexplained trips to Bristol, where they were killed or killed themselves.

Bristol has long been a centre for Soviet espionage activity. Apart from the airport and the docks, it is a major centre for many defence industries, including British Aerospace. It has good motorway links to London, the Midlands and the north. A few miles away lies RAF Brawdy, home of a SOSUS control and information centre (see p 72). Within easy reach are GCHQ at Cheltenham, the Central Government War Operations Centre at Hawthorne, GCHQ subsidiary at Blakenhill, the Morwenstow signals interception installation run jointly by GCHQ and America's National Security Agency (NSA) at Morwenstow, a naval research unit at Bath, RAF Brize Norton, an important staging post for reinforcements to the British Army of the Rhine, the biological defence research establishment at Porton Down and nuclear power stations at Berkeley, Oldbury and Hinkley Point. It was at Bristol that master atom spy Klaus Fuchs, who died in East Germany in January 1988, started the espionage career which delivered the secret of the Manhattan Project to the GRU. Ever since, the university has proved fruitful ground for a variety of Marxist and other extreme left-wing groups.

Despite all these links, and the obvious unresolved questions, Lord Trefgarne (Minister of State for Defence Procurement) replied to Mr Cartwright's letter of concern, as follows. 'I agree that it is odd that all were computer scientists working in the defence field but there any relationship stops. On the information available to me at the moment I do not see that a special enquiry such as you suggest is either desirable or necessary at this time. I shall, however, keep the matter under review.'

A few months later another MP, Mr Doug Hoyle – who is also joint President of the Manufacturing Science Finance Union – called on Defence Secretary Mr Younger to launch an immediate government enquiry into the first three deaths and others which had subsequently come to light, such as that of Mr Roger Hill, a 49-year-old Marconi radar designer who had killed himself with a shotgun for no apparent reason in March 1985. So far as we can ascertain, though, the official line is that there is no need for an enquiry because there is nothing sinister about the deaths and no conspiracy. They are attributed to stress or marital difficulties despite the comments of psychiatrists such as Dr Desmond Kelly mentioned earlier. One journalist, John Sweeney, writing in *The Independent Magazine* on 5 November 1988, even suggested that some of the suicides (if they are suicides) could form part of a 'copycat' syndrome!

One obvious question is how the number of deaths in defence-related industries over the last couple of years compares with the national suicide average for men. Because the statistical sample is so small it is impossible to be precise. Read one way, the figures are below the national average of fourteen suicides per 100,000 men per year, but as Dr Colin Pritchard, head of the psychiatric social work department at Southampton University pointed out in the same magazine article, the figures are 'statistically odd' because defence scientists are carefully screened for mental stability so in theory are less likely to take their own lives than those who do not undergo similar screening. 'It could be a fluke', he commented, 'or there could indeed be something rotten in the state of Denmark.'

Mr Doug Hoyle asked[11] 'What is the link between all these [deaths]? Is it not worrying that this is happening to top scientists? Is it simply overwork, or is there something more sinister afoot? It is very alarming.'

Mr Hoyle's questions followed the death on Friday, 25 March 1988, of another computer expert working for Marconi at Stanmore, 52-year-old Mr Trevor Knight. He was found dead in his car in the garage beneath the maisonette where he had lived for several months after becoming separated from his wife. A hosepipe had been passed from the exhaust into the car. Obviously, this could have been a case of suicide, and we could not begin to claim that all the cases we have studied have anything 'sinister' behind them. It is when they are looked at accumulatively that a pattern emerges, a pattern which screams the message that *something* is going on which cannot be accounted for by the normal law of averages.

*   *   *

With the help of Tony Collins of *Computer News* we have compiled the following details, from which we ask readers to draw their own conclusions, knowing of the GRU's incessant quest for Western scientific and technical knowledge and of the existence of Spetsnaz anti-VIP squads.

The trail begins in March 1982. Professor Keith Bowden, a computer expert at the University of Essex, was killed when his car plunged over an embankment on to a disused railway line. It had crossed the central reservation of the road, near

Witham, without obvious cause. The inquest verdict was one
of accidental death, but the family was not happy and his
widow hired a private investigator whom she claims found
sufficient evidence to suggest that his car had been tampered
with. This was reported to the police but no further action was
taken so far as is known. Professor Bowden acted as a
consultant to Marconi ... In the same year Mr Ernest
Brockway died at his home, apparently of natural causes, and
Mr Jack Wolfenden in a gliding accident. Both men worked
at GCHQ, but there was no suggestion of foul play at the time.
People *do* die of natural causes and accidents, and like Mr
John Cartwright MP, we 'do not wish to be accused of
inventing plots more suited to a television thriller than real
life'. But ...

In 1983 a colleague of Brockway and Wolfenden from
GCHQ, Mr Stephen Drinkwater, was found asphyxiated with
a plastic bag over his head. This is a most unusual form of
suicide, because normally one's body would rebel against the
brain's instructions and force removal of the bag. Most
genuine suicides are accomplished either by painless means
such as a drug overdose or carbon monoxide poisoning in a
car, when the victim slowly sinks asleep; or by fast and
irrevocable means, such as leaping off a high structure. But it
was not the last time a defence scientist died in the same
unusual way, for in January 1987 Mr Richard Pugh, another
Essex man who worked for National Telegraph Systems and
was also an MoD computer consultant, was found dead in his
Loughton home with a plastic bag over his head. His feet were
tied together. The Coroner's verdict was accidental death,
which you might accept if the victim was a small child – but a
grown 37-year-old man?

One possibly acceptable explanation put forward in some
newspaper reports is that Mr Drinkwater was seeking a
bizarre form of sexual stimulation from the effect of partial
suffocation. This is, unfortunately, something quite common,
especially amongst homosexuals. The same is possibly true of
Mark Wismer, a 25-year-old computer expert working for the
Ministry of Defence at Boscombe Down, in Wiltshire, on the
Tornado amongst other projects. In 1987 he asphyxiated
himself by sniffing 'glue' from a sheet of cling-film plastered
over his face. He was wearing woman's boots and PVC
clothing at the time.

Homosexuals, especially married ones whose wives are

unaware of their true inclinations are, of course, particularly susceptible to blackmail. The above three cases could all be genuine accidental deaths – but they could equally well be examples of torture applied to secure information when blackmail failed, and Soviet experience in sophisticated means of torture is well known.

In April 1983 the Commandant of the Royal Military College of Science at Shrivenham, Wiltshire, Lieutenant-Colonel Anthony Godley, vanished. The only apparent reason was that he had had a row with his wife the previous evening. Following his disappearance, his credit cards were used in London and Brussels, but after that the trail went cold. Four years later, in January 1987, Dr John Brittan, a 52-year-old scientist who had formerly worked at the same establishment but was by then employed by the Royal Armament Research and Development Establishment (RARDE) at Chertsey, in Surrey, was found dead in his car. He had locked himself in his garage (or been locked in?) and the engine was still running. In February of the same year Mr Peter Peapell, a 46-year-old lecturer at the Royal Military Academy of Science, was found suffocated beneath his car. He and his wife Maureen had been out for a dinner party and Mr Peapell had told her while she was getting ready for bed that he was just going to put the car away. She found his body the following morning, and the inquest recorded a verdict of accidental death from carbon monoxide poisoning. Mr Peapell had been doing top secret work on new forms of armour protection for tanks and other armoured fighting vehicles, of obvious interest to the Soviet Union.

Lieutenant Robert McGowan was last seen alive on the evening of Monday, 7 November 1988. He was a 22-year-old graduate serving with the Army's Royal Electrical and Mechanical Engineers (REME) and at the time of his death was studying at Shrivenham, making his death the fourth mystery connected with this establishment. On the following morning, 8 November, a friend could get no reply when he knocked on McGowan's door. Two other friends then went outside to the front of the living quarters and one of them managed to climb a drainpipe to reach the first floor balcony. Peering through the window, he saw Lieutenant McGowan's body hanging from a leather belt attached to a hydraulic door spring. Ministry of Defence police broke down the door and removed the body. An Army spokesman said that 'Robert

McGowan's death is a complete mystery and a tragedy. We have no idea what led to it.' Colleagues are equally in the dark. When we contacted the officer's brother at his home in Edinburgh, though, he refused to comment. There was no suicide note.

In 1984 another GCHQ technician, Mr George Franks, was found dead in his Brighton flat. Natural causes were again cited, but some form of poison whose residue quickly evaporates cannot be ruled out. It has been known before, and it takes experts like those at Porton Down to decipher the puzzle, as in the case of Georgi Markov. Then, in November 1985 British Telecom computer expert Jonathan Walsh 'fell' from his hotel balcony in Abidjan, Ivory Coast. The police never satisfactorily established why he had fallen, and although it was suggested he may have been 'high' on unspecified drugs, this was never proven. He was not the first nor the last defence scientist to die in this manner. We have already examined the curious case of Vimal Dajibhai, but even earlier, on 17 June 1983 Mr Dennis Grant Skinner had died of multiple injuries sustained as the result of a fall from his twelfth floor apartment in Leninsky Prospekt, Moscow. The British inquest in this case recorded a verdict of unlawful killing – in other words, murder.

Mr Skinner had arrived in Moscow in the late 1960s as a salesman for the computer company ICL, a prestigious and well-paid job. He was given an attractive Russian secretary, Ludmilla, with whom he soon started having an affair and eventually divorced his wife in order to get remarried. This liaison was a pretty obvious 'swallow' entrapment which Skinner acknowledged when he later spoke to the British Embassy. However, Soviet intelligence did not bargain on a genuine attachment arising. So, when Ludmilla told her controller that Skinner could not obtain for the Soviet Union the trade licences for the computers they wanted, an agent known simply as 'Alexis' made a more direct approach. Whether he was KGB or GRU is really immaterial, although in this case the former seems the more likely to us. Whatever, by this time Ludmilla had come to England to live.

About a week before Skinner's death Ludmilla received a telephone call from him in which he said he would be returning to England earlier than planned, and warned her to be careful of 'an enemy to the family' – a British businessman who has never been named. Skinner also sent a note to the

British Embassy in Moscow saying that he knew the identity of a spy in their staff.

When interviewed in a secure room[12] in the Embassy, Skinner said that he knew he was going to be arrested by the Russians on a charge dreamed up by 'Alexis'. The latter had been disciplined, he said, for allowing Ludmilla to leave the country, and his own arrest was to be used as the lever to bring her back. He also told a business colleague the same story.

For whatever reason, Mr Skinner was allowed to leave the Embassy and return to his flat after imparting his information. If his story was believed ... if he had given a name to a Soviet agent in place ... one must ask why was he not given protection?

Four months after Mr Skinner's murder Dr Richard Mold, Director of the Cancer Registry at London's Westminster Hospital, was visiting Moscow on a lecture tour. In a book[13] he subsequently had published, Dr Mold describes how he was visited one evening in his hotel room by two men who burst in uninvited and pinned him to the wall. One called himself 'Tommy' and said he would translate for his companion, 'Yuri'. The men questioned Dr Mold about a supposed new drug designed to protect nuclear power station workers against the effects of radiation poisoning. Dr Mold denied possessing knowledge of any such drug and eventually the men left, after threatening him with 'Hell or high water if I even told my wife' about the incident.

What frightened Dr Mold was the fact that at one point 'Yuri rose from his perch on the end of the bed, fixed me with a look that said, "sit up and shut up," and walked over to shut the window in my fourth-floor room. This was unnerving since a case had been reported recently of a British merchant banker[14] who fell to his death from a block of flats in Moscow. The whole tenor of this Thursday afternoon's events was one of controlled menace.'

On 10 April 1987 a former colleague of Dennis Skinner, Mr Robert Greenhalgh, fell or was pushed from Brunel's historic road bridge at Sonning Cutting, near Reading. He landed beside the track so avoided being hit by a train but suffered severe head injuries, from which he eventually recovered. He had worked for ICL for fifteen years and had been acquainted with Mr Skinner in the 1970s. His job was determining the requirements of computer systems throughout NATO countries in Europe, a highly sensitive task which he was not

Aircraft are another obvious means for the Warsaw Pact to infiltrate agents and Spetsnaz personnel into the West. Like all Eastern Bloc airliners, the Tupolev Tu-134 – seen here in the livery of Bulgarian Airlines – is basically a military design and would be used in a military role in time of war. Note the nose radome and transparent bomb aimer's position in the nose and the electronic counter-measures pod on top of the tail.

Close-up of an Aeroflot Tu-134 at Prague airport. All Soviet airliners carry at least one KGB security officer whose principal task is to counter any hijacking attempt. However, the crew, who have access in and out of the airport grounds, could well include Spetsnaz personnel tasked with reconnoitring airport layouts and access roads, etc, ready for a time when they may be asked to take them over – as actually happened at Prague, of course.

The archetypal Soviet female officer, Lieutenant Olga Dvoretskanya is a member of the militia and probably in the KGB or GRU. She also holds master's certificates in driving, sambo holds (sambo is a Soviet form of judo) and pistol shooting.

The burnt-out wreck of David Sands' car after he drove it into a cafe wall at 80 mph after loading it with two five-gallon petrol drums.

Police on the scene after Jan Pniok incinerated himself on the same spot as Shani Warren had last been seen. Is there a link?

Demonstrators outside Greenham Common close in on a cruise missile vehicle. If *Jane's Defence Weekly* is correct, they have been infiltrated by Spetsnaz. Police try to reason with a demonstrator on the cab of a cruise missile control vehicle.

Above Demonstrators block the vehicle's exit from Greenham after splattering it with paint.

Below Dutch Army conscripts at a nuclear disarmament rally.

Bottom The links between the various peace campaign organizations and terrorism are well established. Here, Abdalah Frangi, a PLO spokesman, addresses a West German rally, Easter 1988.

allowed to discuss outside the company. He refuses to talk about the incident and now has a full-time plainclothes bodyguard.

Two other cases of deaths in falls are those of 53-year-old Donald Godward, a physicist at the Atomic Weapons Establishment at Aldermaston, and Mr Peter Lebbell, a recruitment consultant for a computer agency. In Godward's case there is no suggestion of foul play – he was walking with his wife while on holiday in Scotland when he slipped and fell a hundred feet down a steep gorge. Mr Lebbell, however, was found by a lorry driver after having fallen – or been pushed – from the top of a multi-storey car park in Slough on 26 April 1988. He was still alive but died from his injuries after arrival at hospital. He had been speaking to his wife on the telephone only minutes beforehand and there was no apparent motive for suicide. In his position as a consultant with the MSL company, Mr Lebbell was well placed to know the names of computer scientists working on defence related projects, which would have been useful information to the GRU.

Another case we investigated, like Mr Godward's, provides 'negative' evidence which adds weight to the suspicious circumstances surrounding others. In April 1987 yet another Marconi employee, 46-year-old Mr Victor Moore, died from an overdose of Paracetamol tablets. He was a design engineer at the company's Space and Defence Systems branch in Portsmouth who, it was said at the inquest, had enjoyed working on weather satellite research but deplored defence projects. He had applied for early retirement when put on a task involving a new night vision device for the Army, but his application had not been accepted and he had been given three months' notice instead. His ex-wife gave testimony to the effect that he drank heavily, was abusive and had strangled one of her Burmese cats! Even so, an element of doubt must remain. Could he have been blackmailed after he was transferred to weapons research, tried to take retirement as a means of being genuinely unable to provide a foreign agency with information, and committed suicide when he was fired instead, with obvious loss of benefits? These are the type of questions to which an official enquiry should address itself.

Three car crashes in 1987 fuelled our own enquiry.

Michael Baker was employed by Plessey on digital defence networks, and in his spare time was a signaller in the Territorial Army's Special Air Service Regiment. His BMW unaccountably veered across the central reservation of a dual carriageway and he was killed outright. His mother said he had had a visitor shortly beforehand, a man she did not know. George Kountis' BMW crashed in the River Mersey, his body being found under the overturned vehicle when the tide went out. He was working on a computer science research programme for IBM at Bristol Polytechnic. Another undergraduate specializing in computers at the Royal College, Stuart Goody, was killed in a car crash while on holiday on Cyprus. Inconclusive, of course, but all possible pieces in the jigsaw.

In October 1987 Mr Martin Hancock, 24, was killed when his car crashed after two youths in a passing car hurled a brick through his windscreen. The youths were caught and 17-year-old Dean Ledger was convicted of manslaughter, but what could their motive have been? Just a stupid prank which went tragically wrong? Mr Hancock was an electronics research scientist working on defence projects.

Earlier in the year, in May 1987 the body of 22-year-old Geoffrey Titley was found lying on his bed with a knife protruding from its chest. Mr Titley had been studying computer sciences at IBM at Husley, near Romford, as part of a full-time industrial training course through North Staffordshire Polytechnic. He was considered brilliant at his work but since returning from the Easter Bank Holiday weekend had become withdrawn and his work had suffered. In his hand when the body was discovered was a note reading 'kill myself tonight ... with a knife', so the inquest recorded a verdict of suicide even though no motive ever emerged. But it is another very strange way in which to kill oneself, and Soviet recruitment of university students goes back decades.

On the evening of that same Easter Saturday the bound body of a young woman was discovered in the shallows of an artificial lake alongside the A4 near her home in Stoke Poges. She was identified as Miss Shani Warren, a 26-year-old secretary employed by the GEC subsidiary Microscope. On Good Friday she had mown the lawn of the house which she shared with two other girls and had loaded the clippings into black plastic sacks to take to her parents' home nearby. She never arrived. Instead, she drove off at about 6.00 pm for twenty minutes in the opposite direction.

Her body was discovered at between six and seven o'clock on Saturday night by Mrs Marjorie Arnold, who was out walking her dog. Mrs Arnold subsequently testified that when she was sailing on the lake the following day, Easter Sunday, she observed a man watching the police investigating the scene. He was very swarthy and stocky in build and had a light-coloured Ford Escort.

Two other witnesses came forward, one of them as the result of an appeal on the BBC television *Crimewatch* programme, Mrs Sandra Organ. On Good Friday she had been driving along the A4 and had stopped in the layby to allow her small daughter to go to the toilet. She saw a woman near the lake carrying black dustbin bags and noticed dropped grass clippings on the ground. Her daughter called out 'Hello!' and the woman turned, smiled and waved. Another 'expensive looking' car was parked near Shani Warren's black Vauxhall Cavalier, later identified as a green BMW or Mercedes. There was a briefcase on the rear shelf and the driver, a man in his thirties dressed in a suit, walked over and talked to the woman. Mrs Organ thought nothing more of the incident until the *Crimewatch* appeal, when it became obvious that the woman she had seen was Shani.

At 1.30 am on Saturday morning lorry driver Mr Donald Ward had stopped in the same layby and later testified that he saw Shani's car as well as two men whom he thought were out jogging. At that time of night?

Shani was wearing tight jeans, a T-shirt and body warmer. Her wrists were bound behind her back with jump leads and her legs with a towing rope, while a scarf gagged her. She had not been sexually assaulted and the only sign of a struggle was bruising around her neck which the Home Office pathologist, Dr Benjamin Davis, concluded had been caused by an attempt to strangle her using the jump leads. The driver's seat in her car was in the reclining position. The actual cause of death, though, was given as drowning. Dr John Hamilton, consultant psychiatrist and Medical Director of Broadmoor Hospital, said that examination of Shani's diaries had shown no psychological abnormalities suggesting she might have been suicidal.

Inside Shani's car police found three empty plastic sacks, her watch and cigarette lighter, a woman's jacket and an Easter Egg. Her purse and a distinctive key ring with a wooden 'Scotland' souvenir tag were missing and have never been found. The keys may have included one for her place of work. When we telephoned Microscope, however, their spokesman was unwilling to discuss the case or tell us the exact nature of Shani's work, not wishing to cause further distress to her family, but Microscope *do* undertake defence related projects.

There was a macabre sequel to the Shani Warren case. In March 1988 the charred body of a man was found on the back seat of a blue Volvo parked in exactly the same spot as Shani's Vauxhall had been. The car had caught fire, although *how* has not been established. The man was identified through dental records as Jan Pniok, a 39-year-old Polish engineer who had emigrated to Britain in 1979. He had no defence connections, working as a storekeeper for H. Leverton, an engineering company making parts for caterpillar tractors, engines and fork-lift trucks. Mr Pniok had no financial worries since he had received £80,000 industrial compensation for an injury to his right hand. Was there any connection between the two cases, or was the second death in the same layby a coincidence?

The year 1988 saw several other strange deaths.

On Monday, 18 January, a nuclear technician working at the Harwell Atomic Energy Establishment disappeared. Russell Smith, aged 23, missed his day release course at nearby Abingdon Technical College on the Tuesday. A police helicopter was called in to help search the snow-covered landscape but nothing was found until 1 February, when his body was recovered from a ledge on cliffs at Williapark, near Boscastle in Cornwall. His father said he had no worries at home or at work.

In February 1988 50-year-old Dr Colin Fisher was stabbed to death by a colleague, Mrs Georgina Stuart. He was a top-ranking nuclear physicist at the Rutherford Laboratories in Chilton, where he had worked for more than twenty years. He was internationally known for his work on particle emissions. Mrs Stuart took an overdose of drugs after killing him, but then called the police. After she had recovered in hospital she was charged with his murder. A romance gone sour? Or did Mrs Stuart have another motive? Colleagues of Dr Fisher said they knew of no relationship other than work between the two, and a neighbour of Mrs Stuart's, Mr Wood, said Dr Fisher had *not* been a frequent visitor at her house. Friends and colleagues usually know when two people are having an affair, no matter how discreet they try to be.

On 10 June the body of a man who has not been named was discovered in a parked car near the tiny village of Six Mile

Bottom, near Newmarket. A suicide note said he had decided to commit suicide because working with radiation had ruined his eyes. The only other information given out was that he came from Pontefract in Yorkshire.

On 23 August 60-year-old Assistant Marketing Director John Ferry apparently placed two wires plugged into the mains in his company flat into his mouth and was electrocuted. He was a senior executive at the Marconi Command and Control Centre in Frimley, Surrey, with an excellent seven-year record. Before that he had risen to the rank of Brigadier in the Army and had a high security clearance, making frequent trips to Washington. He was described by colleagues as a workaholic who treated his staff as though they were in the Army too! No motive for suicide emerged and the Surrey Coroner, Mr Michael Burgess, recorded an open verdict. However, Brigadier Ferry's wife Ann believes it actually was suicide and says that her husband had suffered a complete personality change after a car accident a few weeks earlier. But, Coroner Burgess also recorded an open verdict on the similar death on August Bank Holiday Sunday of Mr Alastair Beckham.

Mr Beckham was employed as an engineer by Plessey naval systems. On the day in question he had driven his wife to work – she had a part-time job as a nurse – taken his dog for a walk and bought the Sunday paper. He was supposed to have picked his wife up from work at two o'clock, but when he failed to turn up she made her own way home. There she found him dead in the garden shed. He had similarly electrocuted himself, bypassing the fuse with a paper clip. A handkerchief was stuffed in his mouth …

Another Bank Holiday death was that of 43-year-old Mr Michael Williams, who worked as a computer programmer for the Home Office at Horseferry House. Earlier in his career, he had been on the team which established the Police National Computer. He had lived in Highgate all his life, had been happily married for eighteen years, and had a two-year-old daughter to whom he was devoted. Mr Williams had been under some pressure of work and was looking forward to a rest over the holiday. On the Friday afternoon he telephoned his wife and said that he would not be home until about 8.00 pm because he was joining colleagues in a pub for a couple of drinks. In fact he lost track of time and it was not until much later that he and a friend boarded their Victoria Line tube train.

The friend got off the train at Victoria, the last person who knew Mr Williams to see him alive, although a ticket collector at East Finchley station remembered seeing someone answering his description at about 12.30 am. At 6.00 am on Saturday a man was walking his Alsatian dog in Highgate Woods. The animal is normally quiet and non-aggressive but on this morning it bounded away immediately it was let off its lead and began barking furiously. Rounding a corner in the path the dog's owner saw it barking at a man who was standing motionless beside a tree. 'He seemed to be hypnotised – staring into the distance,' the owner said later.

The BBC's *Crimewatch* programme staged a reconstruction which showed a man about six feet tall, of slim build and with longish brown hair and a beard. He stood rigidly, totally ignoring the dog. Most people would have reacted differently to a madly barking Alsatian. Standing motionless and showing no signs of either fear or aggression is a technique taught in the police and armed forces – especially the special forces – for dealing with guard dogs.

The owner patted his dog on its head to calm it down and led it away to continue their walk.

Later that morning, at approximately 7.40 a lady, also walking her dog, discovered the dead body of Michael Williams lying beside the path. Police established that the body must have been placed there between 7 and 7.40. He had been killed expertly by a single karate chop to the throat. A police spokesman told us that they were not ignoring the fact that specialist military personnel are trained to react to dogs in the way described, that the single karate blow *could* be laid at the door of a specially trained person, and also admitted that a person working for the Home Office could be a target.

At the time of writing the man seen earlier in the park had not been identified.

Other recent deaths include Andrew Hall, a 33-year-old British Aerospace executive who was found dead in his car during the last week of September with a pipe leading into the vehicle from the exhaust. The Maidenhead Coroner recorded an open verdict. Mr Edwin Skeels had died in just the same way in February 1987. He was an engineer working for Marconi in Leicester on a flight simulation project for the Ministry of Defence. The explanation given at the inquest for recording a verdict of suicide in his case was that Marconi had failed to win the contract for the project and Mr Skeels had been told no further funds would be forthcoming for his work. However, the family do not accept the verdict. His cousin, Ray Palmer, told *Sunday Times* reporters Jon Craig and Barrie Penrose that 'Nobody could believe it. He was very level-headed.'

The family are also suspicious at the death, apparently through a heart attack, of Mr Frank Jennings in June 1987. An engineer working on classified defence projects for Plessey, he was considered to be in good health and, according to colleagues, an unlikely candidate for a heart condition. A woman colleague told Craig and Penrose that she was 'not alone in believing his death may be connected to the sensitive defence work he was doing'. 'Plessey officials', she added, 'searched his house and removed documents after he died.'

The same report also quoted Dr Max Atkinson, author of the book *Discovering Suicide*[15] and a former Senior Research Fellow at the Centre for Socio-Legal Studies, Wolfson College, Oxford, as saying that 'Many coroners are not legally or medically trained. There are a lot of cases, car accidents especially, which get passed off as accidents, but could be either suicides or homicides.'

What is clear is that the deaths are mounting up and renewed pressure is expected to be put on Home Secretary Douglas Hurd – including pressure from a worried Pentagon – for a thorough enquiry to either establish or finally lay to rest the conspiracy theory. Despite his instruction to police authorities in 1987 to liaise over these deaths, so far no link has been publicly acknowledged. Our own connection is simple: Moscow. And it will be interesting to see whether the spate of deaths over the last couple of years diminishes now that Mr Gorbachev has pulled some of the KGB's teeth by appointing in Mr Kryuchkav a new Director who for the first time in that organization's history is not a full member of the Soviet governing body, the Politburo.

Notes Chapter Eight

[1] Roger Boar and Nigel Blundell, *The World's Greatest Spies and Spymasters*, Octopus Books.

[2] *The Guardian*, 27 June 1988.

[3] *The Daily Express*, 27 January 1988.

[4] *The Sunday Telegraph*, 27 March 1988.

[5] Soviet scientific officers in foreign embassies are actually employed by the GRU's 9th Directorate – see Chapter Three.

[6] *The Sunday Times*, 2 October 1988.

[7] *Hansard*, 23 March 1987, page 6.

[8] *ibid*, 25 March 1987, page 159.

[9] *ibid*, 31 March 1987, page 445.

[10] *ibid*, 8 April 1987, page 293.

[11] *The Daily Telegraph*, 28 March 1988.

[12] ie, one protected against electronic or other forms of 'bugging'.

[13] *Mold's Medical Anecdotes*, published by Adam Hilger.

[14] At the time of his death Mr Skinner was representing the Midland Bank.

[15] Macmillan, 1978.

Chapter Nine
Conspiracy

Senator Joseph McCarthy probably did his own cause an even greater disservice than is generally recognized. By his hysterical 'reds under the beds' fanaticism he made it far more difficult for anyone else to discuss the problem of communist infiltration in Western society rationally, without being tarred with the same brush. This, of course, works to the advantage of the Warsaw Pact nations, whose operations can in many cases be carried out more openly because anyone who points an accusing finger at them may lay himself open to ridicule. This is a risk and a challenge we have to accept. It is particularly difficult because it is virtually impossible to pin down the extent of Spetsnaz activity in a documentary fashion which would stand up in a court of law. That there is circumstantial evidence in plenty we have established, and various European governments have admitted there is a problem even if they are shy of discussing it.

We have established that 'support groups', for want of a better term, are already established in Western democracies, ready to lend local knowledge and advice to Spetsnaz reconnaissance, sabotage and murder squads. One of the principal tasks of DI5 (formerly MI5) and Special Branch is keeping track of the membership, motivation and methods of politically left-wing orientated groups in the UK and elsewhere. A large number of such organizations are certainly 'clean' in the sense that they do not take orders from Moscow, but others are definitely suspect. Some, by self-admission, have a membership which is communist by declaration and intent. Others have limited goals – the achievement of a particular type of political, social or environmental change which is in itself innocuous but which unwittingly forms part of the larger pattern being manipulated from behind the Churchillian 'Iron Curtain'. Still others have broader objectives, including the total overthrow of Western governments. Some, as in South Africa, gain adherents from all parts of the political spectrum because their quarrel is with a regime which denies the greater part of its population ordinary civil rights and personal dignity.

Many of these organizations openly endorse the use of violence in the achievement of their aims, such as the various terrorist groups from the PLO and IRA down to the El Salvador and Nicaragua Solidarity Campaigns, for example. Others, while purportedly opposing violence, work indirectly for the same cause by creating a general public reaction against them, a reaction which can itself result in violence. Inner city race riots are an example. For the most part, the members of such organizations are loyal citizens of their country who abhor violence and seek to achieve their desired reform(s) through due process of law and public opinion. But within their ranks lie concealed a hard core of men and women who wish to see nothing less than the total overthrow of 'capitalism' and Western society as we know it, and are prepared to use any means to that end.

There *are* injustices, social, economic and political faults and failures, weaknesses and unfair privileges within Western society, but they are on nothing like the scale which exists within the Soviet Union and its satellites. Perhaps Mr Gorbachev will achieve some genuine internal reforms. He has already downgraded the status of the KGB – on the surface at least – but the average Soviet citizen is still heavily restricted in where he can travel or seek employment; still has to keep curb on his tongue and on what he writes; and can still be imprisoned or sent to a *gulag* without fair public trial. The same is true in some Western countries, of course, because in terms of human rights there is nothing to choose between a government of the far left or of the far right. What the Soviet Union does, through the KGB, GRU, MVD and Spetsnaz, is exacerbate existing problems in other countries and try to foment further discontent aimed at undermining 'the establishment' in order to create an environment in which a Moscow-style rule may become to be seen as preferable. The exact place of Spetsnaz in this is as yet unclear but one example is its activity within CND, the Campaign for Nuclear Disarmament.

As long ago as as January 1986 a British Member of Parliament, Sir Peter Blaker, asked the Prime Minister, Mrs Margaret Thatcher, whether she had seen an article in the magazine *Jane's Defence Weekly* stating that Soviet-trained agents had infiltrated the ranks of the women picketing outside Greenham Common, one of the two acknowledged UK bases for Tomahawk ground-launched cruise missiles. Mrs Thatcher replied that 'government bodies' were aware of the 'implications of special forces operations' and that this was the principal reason behind the exercise 'Brave Defender' (see page 41). What Yossef Bodansky, a Washington correspondent of *Jane's* actually said was as follows:

'The Soviet Union has maintained a secret detachment of female Spetsnaz special forces in the area of Britain's Greenham Common Air Base since … December 1983.

'Soviet defectors have disclosed that three to six trained agents, from Warsaw Pact and West European countries, including the UK, infiltrated women's protest groups at Greenham Common and were present "at all times".'

His report continued to say that 'There has been a regular rotation of agents to enable a large number to gain field experience. The operation is controlled by the GRU …

'The women agents are trained in camps situated in the Rovno-L'vov-Lutsk area of the Carpathian and the Ural and Volga military districts. They contain mock-ups of elements of the Greenham Common camp like the heavily defended inner defence zone[1]. There the women are trained to attack the missile sites under war or surprise conditions in a pre-emptive strike. They will act as "beacons" for other Spetsnaz and airborne troops who would be used to attack the missiles in war.

'These Spetsnaz women receive emergency cash via "dead drops" when needed or they travel abroad to meet their paymasters. The members of the network "holiday" overseas to meet a controller – those who go to Austria go on to Czechoslovakia for a meeting; others who reach Yugoslavia, enter Bulgaria.

'The initial purpose is to incite protesters to mount protests and demonstrations to test the defending forces' reaction times and to monitor security arrangements and timings of cruise missile convoys leaving Greenham.'

A follow-up article said that 'Soviet pre-occupation with the need to neutralize NATO's European-based nuclear weapons dates from the late 1960s when … 'Spetsnaz sub-units and detachments were organized in the Western Military Districts of the USSR for pre-emptive strikes against such targets'.

Naturally, the Greenham women denied these allegations as a slur to discredit them, and the police have said that, despite all the arrests they have made, they have not discovered anyone carrying an Eastern Bloc passport. This, of course, is no more than you would expect; no Soviet operative is going to give himself or herself away so obviously. But Soviet involvement with CND and other Western peace organizations goes back a long way. In 1987 two founder members of CND, Mr Michael Randle and Mr Patrick Pottle, were accused of having masterminded the escape of Soviet spy George Blake from Wormwood Scrubs in 1966, and were interrogated by Special Branch. The two men had met Blake while themselves imprisoned for anti-nuclear activities, and other members of CND were also implicated although no charges were brought. They still refuse to say how the rescue of a maximum security prisoner serving 42 years for spying against his country was effected, though.

A classic example of a Soviet infiltration exercise was unearthed – literally – in 1980. A Welsh farmer, Goronwy Morris, stopped to examine a metal box which had been revealed by his plough. It turned out to contain a Russian radio transmitter, with forty preset frequency plugs all clearly labelled in English. What on earth was it doing buried on a remote Welsh hillside? It was of 1960s' make but in perfect condition.

When this information was revealed by the then Home Secretary, Mr Willie Whitelaw, in March 1981, it did not take journalists long to unearth the fact that ten years earlier, in spring 1971, a party of six Russians – four men, a woman and a small boy – had stayed at the nearby Wynnstay Arms hotel in the village of Llanrhaeadr-ym-Mochnant, Clwyd. The hotel landlord, Mr James Kimpton, dug out the register for the period which revealed that the woman was married to one of the four men, who gave his name as A.P. Savronov. Two of the other men registered under the names Kolushenko and Bourinov. The fourth man refused to sign the register even when asked twice.

Mr Savronov was one of 105 Soviet diplomats expelled from

the UK later in 1971 for what Foreign Secretary Sir Alec Douglas-Home described as 'unacceptable activities' – diplomatic jargon for espionage.

Hotel landlord Kimpton, and his Estonian-born wife Asta, told reporters that the Russian party behaved very strangely for a group on holiday, staying in the hotel all day. But three of the men left at nightfall and drove away carrying a parcel, returning a few hours later.

On 2 April 1981 the 'elder statesman' of espionage journalism, Mr Chapman Pincher, was quoted by *The Guardian* as saying that 'almost certainly the set belonged to an English subversion unit recruited by the KGB [or GRU, of course] for sabotage action in the event of a sudden attack by the Soviet Union. That is why the instructions for using it were in English.' On the same day *The Daily Mail* also quoted Mr Pincher as saying that if the radio had been for use by Soviet agents, 'the instructions would have been in Russian. When I saw the set it was in excellent condition which would not have been the case if it had been buried for ten years without attention.

'The subversive unit would have unearthed it at least once a year to make a check call back to Moscow and replace any parts that were worn. This is regular practice for some 400 subversive units operating out of West Germany. I am afraid it is also happening here, although no-one wants to admit it.'

Britain and Germany are not, naturally, alone in having their 'peace movements' and other subversive groups. In November 1987 protesters broke into the site of a proposed Dutch missile base at Woensdrecht and even penetrated into the underground silos which were still under construction. What disturbed the Dutch authorities was the fact that not only were the protesters able to gain access so easily, but that among their numbers were members of the Dutch armed forces *in uniform*[2]. The Dutch government subsequently took the unprecedented step of buying press, radio and television coverage to say that in future such installations would be defended by the use of force if necessary and that the guards would be authorized to shoot. A similar situation exists in West Germany, although to a lesser degree. There, instead of serving as a conscript for eighteen months, a conscientious objector can opt instead for twenty months' community service (*Zivil Dienst*). On 18-19 March 1988 the 'Zivis', as they are known, staged a rash of anti-nuclear protests throughout Germany. Members of the armed forces joined in, although not in uniform. Many were members of the German Communisty Part (DKP) and the organization 'Socialist Youth of Germany', two groups which have been gaining ground steadily over the last couple of years. Their ultimate aim is German reunification, but in a country ruled from Leipzig rather than Bonn.

What such reports – particularly the CND ones – coupled with the published evidence of various defectors over the years, help to reinforce is the fact that Warsaw Pact 'sleepers', both 'illegals' and 'agents', have been established in the West for decades, the majority living out their lives in peaceful obscurity without ever being called upon to undertake any specific military task. They are given initial funds to establish legitimate businesses, preferably ones which give them an opportunity for travel; they make friends, chat to neighbours and shopkeepers, and are accepted as part of the community until something gives them away. This is usually either because they have been 'activated' for a particular mission which draws attention to them, or because they are betrayed by a defector – every espionage agent's nightmare.

An agent may be an ideological sympathizer, someone who is being blackmailed or a person who has been seduced by a 'raven' or a 'swallow', male and female sexual and emotional predators. More often than not they will not be 'spies' nor even connected with any security-conscious organization, but they will be in place, securely entrenched and ready to lend a hand when called upon, as in the case of those who 'sprang' George Blake. They will be of varying ages. Some will end up as retired couples living in the heart of the countryside where they are well placed to give succour to Spetsnaz operatives before or after a raid. Some will run small hotels and lodging houses where Spetsnaz operatives can hide out without drawing attention. Others will be young and successful business executives or secretaries with flats or houses in major cities. Some will be active in politics, others will behave as if they are politically indifferent. Some will belong to activist groups of one sort or another, but the majority will probably not, for they have to avoid rather than attract attention. And yet, of course, there are two ways of concealing something, and one of the favourite ways has always been to put it on such prominent display that it becomes invisible. The best way to lie is to tell the truth but in such a fashion that people do not believe you.

Some agents will obviously be situated in the proximity of sensitive installations, military or industrial. Much information can be gathered from the idle chat of a coffee morning or after a few drinks at a party. Isolated scraps of information, when collated with other seemingly innocuous items in KGB and GRU computers, can reveal a larger pattern or give meaning to an unknown factor. 'The walls have ears' was a wartime catchphrase which is still appropriate, but in these days of electronic eavesdropping virtually nowhere is safe. Recent cases of 'hacking', of electronics whiz-kids breaking through into secret computer files, prove this beyond doubt.

'Sleepers' are normally self-supporting. They do not, once they are in place, rely upon funds which could be traced, nor do they have a regular contact schedule, but each has a controller with whom they can get in touch in case of an emergency or if a particularly juicy snippet of information comes their way. Each controller will normally have knowledge of more than one agent, but the agents themselves will usually be unknown to each other. They might, for example, work alongside each other in a factory production line but still be unsuspecting. In this way, each acts as a check on the information supplied by the other, so their controller will be able to spot if one has been 'turned'.

Although there has been ample evidence over the years of KGB infiltration and subversion of trades unions in the West, this is not believed to be a Spetsnaz function. The GRU, and Spetsnaz, are military organizations concerned with military technology and only indirectly with politics. However, the existence of organizations such as Militant must act in the Soviet special forces' favour, providing a ready base of sympathizers potentially ready to lend assistance to operative teams. Large numbers of these extreme left-wing sympathizers work in various capacities within the Civil Service[3] and there are undoubtedly others within the police, fire brigade, hospital, telephone and postal and other vital services. Although not employed in militarily sensitive positions, such people will have access to information which could be invaluable to a Spetsnaz team.

Militant is only one of over a hundred organizations in the UK which could be of assistance to Spetsnaz in time of need. Apart from overtly political groups such as the Communist Party of Great Britain (CPGB), these include gay and black rights movements and environmental pressure groups from the African National Congress (ANC) down to the Quaker Peace Group, to cite two extreme examples. It would be pointless to list them all and the majority of members of, for example, the Youth Training Scheme or the Manpower Services Commission would be horrified to find that their organizations are among those whose activities fall within Special Branch's watching brief, and probably even more horrified to discover that they exist on a list which also includes the English Collective of Prostitutes ... Virtually any organization with a social role or which promotes a minority group against which discrimination exists is vulnerable to Eastern Bloc activists, provocateurs and agents, even though the majority of their members are patently innocent of any form of subversive activity. We do not wish to reincarnate Senator McCarthy, but our researches clearly indicate that this is the case.

There is a strong tradition of anarchist groups in the United Kingdom, and although the cartoon image of the black-garbed figure carrying a bomb with a spluttering fuze has passed into history, there is disturbing evidence for the existence of more than one hardline group which openly promotes violence to disrupt society. As in West Germany, it will be upon such groups that Spetsnaz teams may rely for local assistance and 'cannon fodder'. In 1987 the international revolutionary solidarity movement, the First of May Group, published a detailed handbook of guerrilla tactics for use against the police and other establishment authorities. The handbook was published anonymously in the Orkneys. A similar, shorter manual entitled *Without a Trace* was produced abroad and smuggled into left-wing bookshops in the UK by the extremist Hurricane group, which was implicated in the disturbances in Wapping aimed against Mr Rupert Murdoch's new newspaper works.

Topics covered in these booklets include intelligence, and how to acquire stolen or forged identity documents. They make recommendations about firepower, stressing the need for guerrilla groups to standardize their weaponry to ensure ammunition commonality, showing the advantage of larger calibre hand guns, and giving advice on converting commercially available sporting guns for military purposes. There are sections on behaviour during interrogation and in prison. 'Do not be deceived by the "friendly" approach', the First of May Group publication says.

'This is only a technique to throw you off your guard – their true face will be revealed soon enough.' If force is being used, the booklet says, 'Don't attempt to remain upright. Play the role of "dead" or "injured". Fall onto the floor and roll onto your stomach. In this position, kicking and clubbing cause less damage. Also attempt to pull in your chin and attempt to protect the kidneys by pulling in your elbows.'

Describing the role of civilian 'action groups', the booklet says that

'Although the civilian resistance acts mainly as an urban rearguard providing logistical support, new personnel and an information system ... the guerrilla movement itself will sometimes have to carry out specific actions. These might be to free an imprisoned member of the guerrilla units, to free hostages, capture files or destroy key industrial installations and transportation facilities.

'All participants in the action who are employed should have a valid reason for staying off work with a suitable document from a doctor (who will probably also be part of the civilian resistance).

'In a larger city the sewage system should be prepared as a hiding place should things go wrong. It should be stocked with food, drink, first aid equipment, clothes, ammunition, maps, etc.'

The booklet goes on to describe how to occupy houses and shops in the vicinity of the target, plan escape routes and block the security forces' communications and routes of access. Similarly, the Hurricane group publication gives advice on neutralizing police video cameras by aiming flashguns at them and, ominously, gives a list of police radio call signs and shows how to recognize unmarked police cars. Earlier, the group had also circulated a list of over 100 prominent businessmen and politicians specifically targetted for attack. Nor is this the only such list.

In February 1988 *The Sunday Times* spotlighted an internal document circulated to members of the ultra-left Workers Revolutionary Party listing prominent Jewish citizens in Britain who are targets for attack. The names included Sir Keith Joseph and Leon Brittan, MP. The

Workers Revolutionary Party is, said *The Sunday Times*, financed primarily by Colonel Gaddafi of Libya with other funds coming from Abu Dhabi, Iraq, Kuwait, the Palestine Liberation Organization, Qatar and other unidentified sources. Here, as in other areas of endeavour, the KGB and GRU are using 'fellow travellers' in countries outside the Warsaw Pact to finance, support and provide training facilities for revolutionary guerrilla groups in NATO countries. Extremists come from all over the world to train in special camps set up in Libya and other Middle Eastern and North African states, including Afghanistan, Ethiopia, Iraq, South Yemen and Syria. The military side of this training is conducted by instructors seconded from Spetsnaz. Other training camps are known to exist in Cuba, Angola, Nicaragua and Vietnam, while some IRA members have undergone courses in Czechoslovakia and East Germany. Many of the arms and explosives captured by the security forces in Northern Ireland similarly come from Eastern Bloc sources.

When the United States sent airborne and other special forces units into Grenada in 1982 they captured over 900 Cuban, Russian, North Korean, Libyan, East German and Bulgarian personnel, including a staff of permanent military advisors. Warehouses full of Soviet small arms and ammunition were discovered, far in excess of the requirements of the island's 600 regular army troops.

The truly international scope of the Soviet 'conspiracy' is clearly seen in the existence of a large number of foreign organizations with a strong left-wing bias[4]. As we have said before, the majority of their members are probably perfectly ordinary, law-abiding citizens and most do not toe the Moscow line but within each there exists a hard core of dedicated extremists who will use literally any means to achieve their aims – aims which coincide with Moscow's. Britain is specifically targetted as a centre for revolutionary action. As long ago as 1980 the Foreign Military Review, *Zarubezhnoe Voennoe Obozrenie*, published a strategic survey of the UK spotlighting over a hundred specific targets, military and economic, for attack. Many lie in or close to large towns and cities which provide secure bases for urban guerrillas, many groups of which are already in place ready to help the Spetsnaz teams when called upon to do so. The big question is whether Britain's defences will be adequate to stop them, and exercises such as 'Brave Defender' throw considerable doubt on this.

In time of tension preceding actual military action by the Warsaw Pact, the various groups spread throughout society would aim to cause as much disruption as possible by means of demonstrations, strikes and riots, the aim being to distract and disperse the efforts of the police and security forces. Deliberate sabotage is more than possible, it is inevitable. It may be a relatively simple task to defend a power station against attack, for example, but it would be totally impossible to guard every electricity pylon in the country. Mike Welham, as a former member of the Royal Marines, knows only too well how difficult it is to guard *any* installation against a determined intruder.

'However important guard duty is', he says, 'it is invariably boring. You are probably alone, armed with a weapon and a radio. At a set time, someone will speak to you or you will call in. No matter how keen or good you are, the feeling of loneliness soon creeps in. You check your watches and the minutes drag by. In the early hours of the morning, drowsiness blurs your mind. You want to walk about, stamp your feet,. whistle. Many people do, in fact, whistle or talk to themselves. A feeling that nobody is going to want to attack your installation grows insidiously, that nobody could penetrate the barbed wire anyway so you might as well relax.'

The attitude of the special forces soldier on a penetration mission will be totally different to this. He may be cold, hungry or tired, but he will be keyed up and totally alert. Mike says

'I was a member of a team of four which was tasked with testing the security of a diplomatic radio station. Because of its location, it was a prime target. It was guarded by a company of a premier infantry regiment who were issued with live ammunition. If we were caught we knew we would have to surrender instantly or they would open fire.

'We were given two hours in which to plant dummy explosive charges. Two hours is a long time and it did not take us long to gain access to the steel-railed perimeter fence. We unbolted one rail, which allowed the smallest member of our team to slip through. He carried and placed the clumsy charge inside the building, having crossed an expanse of open and well lit ground without detection. He came out the same way and we returned to our rendezvous. Two other teams also succeeded in planting their charges.'

We have not quoted the above to disparage the security forces, but to show how extremely difficult it really is to guard any installation against determined, skilled and aggressive men, which the Spetsnaz are by any standards.

* * *

The threat from Spetsnaz is very real and very current and they have plenty of potential helpers well entrenched within the fabric of Western society. To over-react to the threat would, however, be as dangerous as pretending it does not exist. To counter it fully would need stronger methods than those already recently introduced, such as the denial to a terrorist suspect of the right to remain silent. Refusal to answer a question may be seen to imply guilt. This has already been seen by many people, not just of the left, as a potentially serious erosion of civil rights, and further moves along these lines will add to fears of Britain gradually becoming the same sort of police state which the Kremlin would like to impose. But *something* has to be done to control both Soviet espionage operations and the growth of highly dangerous left-wing urban guerrilla groups.

It would be nice to know that the governments of the West *are* aware of the situation and *are* doing something about it ...

Notes Chapter Nine

[1] This is not an isolated fact. The GRU has built several mock-ups of NATO installations, from airfields and missile sites to harbour installations, in order to train Spetsnaz operatives in ways of attacking them. The USSR is not, of course, unique in doing this. Britain's Special Air Service Regiment, for example, trains for its counter-terrorist role in Northern Ireland using replicas of parts of actual town streets.

[2] Members of the Dutch armed forces actually have their own trades union, which is actively campaigning at the present time to make

conscientious objectors exempt from conscription.

[3] 122 activists and 147 sympathizers according to figures supplied by *The Daily Telegraph* Information Bureau in mid-1988.

[4] These include: the Belgian Flemish Action Committee and National Action Committee for Peace and Development; the Dutch No Cruise Missiles Committee which includes members from nine peace groups, seven political parties, the Trades Union Federation and the Union of Conscripted Soldiers; the Third World Group; the Communist Parties of all nationalities; the Moscow Trust Group, Soviet Peace Committee, Czechoslovakian and East German Peace Groups, the World Peace Council (which is KGB sponsored), the World Federation of Democratic Youth and the International Federation of Resistance Fighters. This list is far from exhaustive.

Acknowledgements

The authors would like to thank the following individuals and organizations for their assistance in preparing this book: the *Aberdeen Press and Journal*; the American Defense Preparedness Association; the Armament-Disarmament Unit, Sussex University; Mr John Cartwright, MP; *Computer News*; the Conservative Research Unit; *The Daily Telegraph* Information Bureau; Mr Eric Deakin, MP; Mr Simon Errington; INS News Agency; the Institute for European Defence and Strategic Studies; Mr M. Kielty; Mr Garry Murray; the Norwegian Press Attaché; Mr Kevin Skinner; Slingsby Engineering Ltd; the South African Embassy; the Soviet Research Centre, Royal Military Academy, Sandhurst; Support Documents, Washington DC; the Swedish Ministry of Defence; Mr Graham Sykes; the West German Defence Department; Mr Desmond Wettern and those who wished to remain unnamed but whose input was invaluable.

Select Bibliography

Advanced Technology Warfare, various authors (Salamander, 1985).

After Long Silence, Michael Straight (Collins, 1983).

Andropov, Arnold Beichman and Mikhail S. Bernstam (Stein & Day, 1983).

Atom Bomb Spies, The, H. Montgomery Hyde (Hamish Hamilton, 1980).

Beyond Top Secret, Ewen Montagu, (Peter Davies, 1977).

British Army in Northern Ireland, The, Lieutenant-Colonel Michael Dewar (Arms & Armour Press, 1985).

British Intelligence Services in Action, Kennedy Lindsay (Dunrod Press, 1980).

Climate of Treason, The, Andrew Boyle (Hutchinson, 1979).

Crime against the World, A, Vladil Lysenko (Victor Gollancz, 1983).

Dictionary of Espionage, The, Christopher Dobson and Ronald Payne (Harrap, 1984).

Electronic Warfare, Doug Richardson (Salamander, 1985).

Forty Years of Soviet Spying, Ronald Seth (Cassell, 1965).

GCHQ, Nigel West (Weidenfeld & Nicolson, 1986).

Intelligence War, The, various authors (Salamander, 1983).

KGB, Brian Freemantle (Michael Joseph, 1982).

KGB, Eyes of Russia, The, Harry Rositzke (Doubleday, 1981).

KGB, Secret Work of Soviet Secret Agents, The, John Barron (Reader's Digest Association, 1973).

KGB Today: The Hidden Hand, John Barron (Reader's Digest Association, 1983).

Military Intelligence, John Patrick Finnegan (History Office, US Army Intelligence and Security Command, 1985).

Modern British Army, Encyclopaedia of the, Terry Gander (Patrick Stephens, 1980 and subsequent editions).

Modern Elite Forces, Max Walmer (Salamander, 1984).

Modern Royal Air Force, Encyclopaedia of the, Terry Gander (Patrick Stephens, 1984 and subsequent editions).

Modern Royal Navy, Encyclopaedia of the, Paul Beaver (Patrick Stephens, 1982 and subsequent editions).

Modern Soviet Weapons, Edited by Ray Bonds (Salamander, 1986).

Mole, William Hood (Weidenfeld & Nicolson, 1982).

Penkovsky Papers, The, Oleg Penkovsky, Trs P. Deriabin (Collins, 1965).

Plumbat Affair, The, Elaine Davenport, Paul Eddy and Peter Gillman (André Deutsche, 1978).

Puzzle Palace, The, James Bamford (Sidgwick & Jackson, 1983).

Secret Intelligence in the Twentieth Century, Constantine FitzGibbon (Hart-Davis, MacGibbon, 1976).

Shadow Network, The, Edward Van Der Rhoer (Robert Hale, 1983).

Silent War, The, Richard Deacon (David & Charles, 1978).

Soviet Military Intelligence, Viktor Suvorov (Hamish Hamilton, 1984).

Spetsnaz, Viktor Suvorov (Hamish Hamilton, 1987)

Technology in War, Kenneth Macksey (Arms & Armour Press, 1986).

Technology of Espionage, The, Lauran Paine, (Robert Hale, 1978).

Their Trade is Treachery, Chapman Pincher (Sidgwick & Jackson, 1981).

Thirty Years with the KGB, Leo Heaps (Methuen, 1984).

Too Secret Too Long, Chapman Pincher (Sidgwick & Jackson, 1984).

War Facts Now, Christy Campbell (Fontana, 1982).

World's Greatest Spies & Spymasters, The, Roger Boar and Nigel Blundell (Octopus, 1984).

World's Elite Forces, The, Bruce Quarrie (Octopus, 1985).

World's Secret Police, The, Bruce Quarrie (Octopus, 1986).

Plus various papers published by the Soviet Studies Centre, Royal Military Academy Sandhurst and various magazine and newspaper articles credited in the chapter notes.

Index